By Mary Higgins Clark

Kitchen Privileges
Silent Night/All Through the Night
Mount Vernon Love Story
Daddy's Little Girl
On the Street Where You Live
Before You Say Good-bye
We'll Meet Again
All Through the Night
You Belong to Me
Pretend You Don't See Her
My Gal Sunday
Moonlight Becomes You
Silent Night
Let Me Call You Sweetheart
The Lottery Winner
Remember Me
I'll Be Seeing You
All Around the Town
Loves Music, Loves to Dance
The Anastasia Syndrome and Other Stories
While My Pretty One Sleeps
Weep No More, My Lady
Stillwatch
A Cry in the Night
The Cradle Will Fall
A Stranger Is Watching
Where Are the Children?

By Mary Higgins Clark and Carol Higgins Clark

He Sees You When You're Sleeping
Deck the Halls

Kitchen Privileges

A Memoir

Mary Higgins Clark

SIMON & SCHUSTER

NEW YORK   LONDON   TORONTO   SYDNEY   SINGAPORE

SIMON & SCHUSTER
Rockefeller Center
1230 Avenue of the Americas
New York, NY 10020

Designed by Jan Pisciotta

Manufactured in the United States of America

ISBN 0-7432-0605-3

Acknowledgments

Creating fictional characters is a never-ending challenge but in many ways it is easier than telling the story of my own life. Once again I'm truly grateful to my editor, Michael Korda, and his associate, senior editor Chuck Adams, for the daily guidance, encouragement, and support they offered. Again, and always, one hundred thousand thanks. It's a privilege to work with you.

Eugene Winick and Sam Pinkus, my literary agents, are great in every way. It's always a joy to work with you.

Many thanks to Lisl Cade, a dear friend and marvelous publicist.

Associate Director of Copyediting Gypsy da Silva continues to be eagle-eyed, unflappable, and wise. Love you, Gypsy.

A tip of the hat to my assistants, Agnes Newton and Nadine Petry. Blessings and kudos to my readers-in-progress, my daughter Carol Higgins Clark and my sister-in-law Irene Clark.

Thank you to all my family and friends who helped me to remember the days gone by.

My love and gratitude to my husband, John Conheeney, our children, and grandchildren. They are my Alpha and Omega.

The tale is told—

This writer rejoices.

For my family and friends
Those who live on in my memory
and
Those who still share my life
With love

Kitchen Privileges

The Bronx—me at age four.

PROLOGUE

*I*n the autumn when the trees become streaked with red and gold and the evenings take on the warning chill that winter is coming, I experience a familiar dream. I am walking alone through the old neighborhood. It is early autumn there as well, and the trees are heavily laden with the russet leaves they will soon relinquish. There is no one else around, but I experience no sense of loneliness. Lights begin to shine from behind curtained windows, the brick-and-stucco semi-detached houses are tranquil, and I am aware of how dearly I love this Pelham Parkway section of the Bronx.

I walk past the winding fields and meadows where my brothers and I used to go sleighriding: Joe, the older, setting the pace on his Flexible Flyer, little Johnny clinging to my back as we followed Joe's sled through the twists and turns of the steep sloping field we dubbed Suicide Hill. Jacoby Hospital and the Albert Einstein Medical Center

cover those acres now, but in my dream they do not yet exist.

I walk slowly from the field down Pinchot Place to Narragansett Avenue and pause in front of the house where the Clark family lives. Once again I am sixteen and hoping the door will open and I may just happen to run into Warren Clark, the twenty-five year old whom I secretly adore. But in my dream I know that five years more must pass before we have that first date. Smiling, I hurry along the next block to Tenbroeck Avenue and open the door of my own home.

The clan is around the table, my parents and brothers, aunts and uncles, cousins and courtesy cousins, the close neighbors and friends who have become extended family. There's a kettle whistling, a cozy waiting to keep the teapot warm, and everyone is smiling, glad to be together.

Unseen, I take my place among them as the latest happenings are discussed, the old stories retold. Sometimes there are bursts of laughter, other moments eyes brighten with unshed tears at the memory of this one or that one who had such a terrible time, "never a day's luck in his life." Memories come flooding back as I hear the stories retold of tender love matches, of bad bargains made at the altar and endured for a lifetime, of family tragedies and triumphs.

I can speak for no other author. We are indeed all islands, repositories of our own memory and experience, nature and nurture. But I do know that whatever writing success I have

enjoyed is keyed, like a kite is to string, and string to hand, to the fact that my genes and sense of self, spirit, and intellect have been formed and identified by my Emerald Isle ancestry.

Yeats wrote that the Irish have an abiding sense of tragedy that sustains them through temporary periods of joy. I think that the mix is a little more balanced. During troubled times, they are sure that it will all work out in the end. When the sun is shining, the Irish keep their fingers crossed. Too good to be true, they remind each other. Something's bound to give.

> *Kate. Wasn't it a damn shame about her? The prettiest thing who ever walked in shoe leather, and she chose that one. And to think that she could have had Dan O'Neill. He put himself through law school at night and became a judge. He never married. For him it was always Kate.*
>
> *Anna Curley. She died in the flu epidemic of 1917, a week before she and Jimmy were to be married. Remember how the poor fellow had saved every nickel and had had the apartment furnished and ready for her? She was buried in her wedding dress, and the day of the funeral, Jimmy swore he'd never draw another sober breath. And wasn't he a man of his word?*

The faces begin to fade, and I awaken. It is the present, but the memories are still vivid. All of them. From the beginning. May I share them with you?

My parents, Nora and Luke Higgins, at Rockaway Beach, circa 1923.

ONE

*M*y first conscious memory is of being three years old and looking down at my new baby brother with a mixture of curiosity and distress. His crib had not been delivered on time, and he was sleeping in my doll carriage, thereby displacing my favorite doll, who was ready for her nap.

Luke and Nora, my mother and father, had kept company for seven years, a typical Irish courtship. He was forty-two and she pushing forty when they finally tied the knot. They had Joseph within the year; me, Mary, nineteen months later; and Mother celebrated her forty-fifth birthday by giving birth to Johnny. The story is that when the doctor went into her room, saw the newborn in her arms and the rosary entwined in her fingers, he observed, "I assume this one is Jesus."

Since we weren't Hispanic, in which culture Jesus is a common name, John, the first cousin of the Holy Family, was the

closest Mother could get. Later when we were all in St. Francis Xavier School and instructed to write J.M.J., which stood for Jesus, Mary, and Joseph, on the top of our test papers, I thought it was a tribute to Joe and me and Johnny.

The year 1931, when Johnny made his appearance, was a good one in our modest world. My father's Irish pub was flourishing. In anticipation of the new arrival, my parents had purchased a home in the Pelham Parkway section of the Bronx. At that time more rural than suburban, it was only two streets away from Angelina's farm. Angelina, a wizened elderly lady, would show up every afternoon on the street outside our house, pushing a cart with fresh fruit and vegetables.

"God blessa your momma, your poppa, tella them I gotta lotsa nicea stringabeans today," she would say.

Our house, 1913 Tenbroeck Avenue, was a semidetached six-room brick-and-stucco structure with a second half bath in a particularly chilly section of the basement. My mother's joy in having her own home was only slightly lessened by the fact that she and my father had paid ten thousand five for it, while Anne and Charlie Potters, who bought the other side, had only paid ten thousand dollars for the identical space.

"It's because your father has his own business, and we were driving an expensive new car," she lamented.

But the expensive new car, a Nash, had sprung an oil leak as they drove it out of the showroom. "It was the beginning of our luck going sour," she would later reminisce.

The Depression had set in with grim reality. I remember as

a small child regularly watching Mother answering the door to find a man standing there, his clothes clean but frayed, his manner courteous. He was looking for work, any kind of work. Did anything need repairing or painting? And if not, could we possibly help him out with a cup of coffee, and maybe something to eat.

Mother never turned away anyone. She left a card table in the foyer and would willingly fix a meal for the unexpected guest. Juice, coffee, a soft-boiled egg and toast in the morning, sandwiches and tea for lunch. I don't remember anyone ringing the bell after midafternoon. By then, God help them, they were probably on their way home, if they had a home to go to, with the disheartening news that there was no work to be had.

I loved our house and our neighborhood. Mine was the little room, its window over the front door. I would wake in the morning to the clipclop of the horses pulling the milk and bread wagons. Borden's milk. Dugan's bread and cake. Sights that have passed into oblivion as surely as the patient horses and creaking wagons that teased me awake and comforted me with their familiarity all those years ago. A box was in permanent residence on the front steps of our house to hold the milk bottles. In the winter, I used to gauge the temperature by checking to see if the cream at the top of the bottles had frozen, forcing the cardboard lids to rise.

During the summer, in midafternoon, we'd all be alert for the sound of jingling bells that meant that Eddie, the Good Humor Man, was wheeling his heavy bicycle around the cor-

ner. Looking back, I realize he couldn't have been more than in his early thirties. With a genuine smile and the patience of Job, he waited while the kids gathered around him, agonizing over their choice of flavor.

All of us had the same routine: a nickle on weekdays for a Dixie cup; a dime on Sunday for a Good Humor on a stick. That was the hardest day for making up my mind. I loved burnt almond over vanilla ice cream. On the other hand, I also loved chocolate over chocolate.

Once the choice had been made, the trick for Joe and John and me was to see who could make the ice cream last the longest so that the other guys' tongues would be hanging out as they watched the winner enjoy those final licks. The problem was that on hot Sundays the ice cream melted faster, and it wasn't unusual for the one who made it last the longest to see half the Good Humor slide off the stick and land on the ground. Then the howls of anguish from the afflicted delighted the other two, who now had the satisfaction of chanting, "Ha, ha. Thought you were so smart."

Eddy the Good Humor man had lost the thumb and index finger of his left hand up to the knuckle. He explained that there had been something wrong with the spring of the heavy refrigerator lid, and it had smashed down on those fingers. "But it was a good accident," he explained. "The company gave me forty-two dollars, and I was able to buy a winter coat for my wife. She really needed one."

The Depression didn't really hit our family until I was in

the third or fourth grade. We had a cleaning woman, German Mary, whom we called "Lally" because she would come up the block singing, "Lalalalaaaaa." Years later, she became the model for Lally in my second book, *A Stranger Is Watching.* Back then, she was the first perk to go.

We always had two copies of the *Times* delivered each day. One copy was saved, and I delivered it to the convent on my way to school the next morning. In those days the nuns were not allowed to read the current day's paper. But as times got increasingly tough, they were out of luck. Mother had to cancel the delivery of both papers. I guess when you think about it, the delivery guy was out of luck, too.

I wrote my first poem when I was six. I still have it because Mother saved everything I wrote. She also insisted that I recite everything I wrote for the benefit of anyone who happened to be visiting. Since she had four sisters and many cousins, all of whom visited frequently, I am sure there must have been regular if silent groans when she would announce, "Mary has written a lovely new poem today. She has promised to recite it for us. Mary, stand on the landing and recite your lovely new poem."

When I was finished thrilling everyone with my latest gem, my mother led the applause. "Mary is very gifted," she would announce. "Mary is going to be a successful writer when she grows up."

Looking back, I am sure that the captive audience was ready to strangle me, but I am intensely grateful for that early

vote of absolute confidence I received. When I started sending out short stories and getting them back by return mail, I never got discouraged. Mother's voice always rang in my subconscious. Someday I was going to be a successful writer. I was going to make it.

That's why, if I may, I'd like to direct a few words to parents and teachers: When a child comes to you wanting to share something he or she has written or sketched, be generous with your praise. If it's a written piece, don't talk about the spelling or the penmanship; look for the creativity and applaud it. The flame of inspiration needs to be encouraged. Put a glass around that small candle and protect it from discouragement or ridicule.

I also started writing skits, which I bullied Joe and John into performing with me. I served as writer, director, producer, and star. I remember Johnny's plaintive request, "Can't I ever be the star?"

"No, I wrote it," I explained. "When you write it, you get to be the star."

Mother's unmarried sisters, May and Agnes, were our most frequent visitors and therefore the longest suffering witnesses to my developing talent. May was eleven months older than Mother and, like her, had been a buyer in a Fifth Avenue department store. Ag, the second youngest in the family, fell in love at twenty-four with Bill Barrett, a good-looking, affable detective, fourteen years her senior. There was one fly in the

ointment: old Mrs. Barret, Bill's mother, who spent most of her life with her feet on the couch, had begged Bill not to marry until God called her. She was sure her death was imminent and wanted him under her roof when her time came.

Months became years. Everyone loved Bill, but from time to time I could hear Mother urging Agnes to ask him about his intentions. They had been keeping company for twenty-four years when God finally beckoned a Barrett, but it was Bill, not his mother, who died. At ninety-five she was still going strong. Her other son, who'd been smart enough to marry young, shipped her to a nursing home. Guess who visited her regularly? Agnes.

At seven I was given a five-year diary, one of those leather-bound jobs with four lines allotted for each day and a tiny gold key which, of course, locks nothing. The first entry didn't show much promise. Here it is, in its entirety:

"Nothing much happened today."

But then the pages began to fill, crammed with the day-to-day happenings on Tenbroeck Avenue among friends and family.

When Mother's sisters and cousins and courtesy cousins came to visit, the stories would begin around the dining room table, over the teacups.

Nora, remember Cousin Fred showing up for
your wedding? . . .

Mother had sent an invitation to some remote cousins in Pennsylvania, forgetting that Cousin Fred had a lifetime railroad pass. He and his wife showed up on her doorstep the morning of the wedding, their nine-year-old grandson in tow. The lifetime pass included the family. Mother ended up cooking breakfast for them and having the kid running around the house while she and May dressed.

> *Nora, remember how that fellow you were seeing invited Agnes to the formal dance and Poppa was in a rage? "No man comes into my house and chooses between my daughters," he said.*

I loved the old stories. The boys had no patience for them, but I drank them in with the tea. As long as I didn't fidget, I was always welcome to stay.

Our next door neighbor, Annie Potters, often joined the group. Charlie, a chubby policeman, was Annie's second husband. She'd been widowed during the flu epidemic of 1917, when she was twenty years old. That husband, Bill O'Keefe, rested in her memory as "my Bill." Charlie was "my Charlie." They married when both were in their late thirties.

"I was so lonesome," Annie would reminisce. "Every night I'd cry in my bed for my Bill. But nobody wants to hear your troubles, so I always kept a smile on my face. They called me the Merry Widow. Then I met my Charlie."

Charlie died many years later, at the age of seventy, and two years after that Annie married "my Joe." When God

called him to join his predecessors, Annie began looking around but hadn't connected by the time she was reunited with her spouses.

A woman with a jutting jaw and dyed red hair, Annie had one of the first permanent waves ever given in the Bronx. Unfortunately, when the heavy metal coils were removed, 60 percent of her hair permanently disappeared with them. Nevertheless, when she looked in the mirror, she saw Helen of Troy and conducted herself accordingly. Annie was the model for my continuing character, Alvirah, the Lottery Winner.

At home, the money situation grew tighter, and my father was looking more and more exhausted. His routine had been to sleep until eleven, have brunch, go to "the place," as he called the pub, come home at five o'clock for a family dinner, then go back to the place until three in the morning.

As he had to let one bartender go, then a waiter, and finally the extra bartender, he began to get up earlier and earlier to take over the ordering of supplies and the other details that his employees had formerly handled.

The problem was that in those days people ran tabs. They charged drinks, they charged their dinners, and then they couldn't pay their bills. If credit was refused, they simply went somewhere else where new credit was easily granted in the hope that payment eventually would be made.

Mother said that the people who were lucky were the ones who worked for the government—teachers, firemen, police-men. Maybe that was the reason that when I reached dating

age, her prayer for me was that I'd marry an Irish Catholic with a city job, so I'd always have a pension.

But things were tight even in the city government. Mayor LaGuardia disbanded the Policemen's Glee Club, of which Charley Potters was a charter member. That meant that Charley was back directing traffic and could be heard muttering about how "the fat little midget bastard in City Hall was destroying the city's culture."

Annie's father, Mr. Fitzgerald, lived with his daughter and her husband. Known on the block as Old Man Fitz, he'd sit by the hour on the divider between our stoops, puffing on a pipe, his skinny behind protected by a thick pillow. Every so often he'd moan, "Oh, my God," which if you happened to be passing by was a touch unnerving.

Mother decided that if she rented the little room, my room, it would bring in extra money, and so we took in a boarder. We could not know then that our first roomer was but a preview of coming attractions. She was a slender lady of uncertain age, with pale skin, limpid eyes, and wispy hair that she wrapped in a loose chignon.

Her wardrobe was sufficient to clothe a convention of similarly sized women. Her effects began to arrive the week before she joined us: a steamer trunk, suitcases, hat boxes. I wondered if she thought she had rented the whole house.

Then she arrived, and a problem soon became evident. She began her morning toilette at 5:30 A.M. Back and forth from the little room to the bathroom she flip-flopped on backless

high-heeled sandals. The tub roared. The sink gushed. She flushed the toilet at two minute intervals. It was Joe's theory that she was giving individual pieces of Kleenex a ride through the sewer system.

The bathroom shared a common wall with my father's bedroom. Daddy was already sleep-deprived, so the last thing he needed was our new tenant. She lasted only one week, so I got my little room back again, at least temporarily.

Saturdays we went to the movies. Ten cents bought an afternoon's entertainment consisting of a double-feature, previews of coming attractions, a cartoon, Movietone News ("The eyes and ears of the world") and a Lone Ranger serial.

On the way home, we went to confession, hoping to avoid Father Campbell, who could have headed the Spanish Inquisition. I remember trembling as I confessed that I had looked up a bad word in the dictionary.

The word was "damn," and my curiosity had been aroused by the difference between the damned who were going to hell, and Mother telling Daddy to "give up the damn place before it kills you."

Father Campbell didn't ask what word I'd looked up. He lectured me on using my eyes for sinful purposes.

Johnnie fared a lot better. When he was mad at me and sprinkled sugar over my baked potato, Mother told him to confess because it was a sin to waste food.

He was smart. He went to Father Breen, who was a doll.

"What did Father say when you told him what you had done?" Mother demanded.

"He laughed."

There were three girls on the block who were my constant companions: Mary Catherine, Carolyn, and Jackie. One day we decided to start a club. Mary Catherine was elected president, Caroline vice-president, and I became secretary. That meant that by default Jackie was the only nonofficer.

Seeing the disappointment on her face, I suggested we hold a new election. Unfortunately I didn't present my full plan, which was that we elect Jackie treasurer and then recruit two younger girls, Joan Murphy and Cookie Hilmer, as dues-paying members.

We had the new election, and I became the only member without a title. At the age of ten, I learned that sometimes we can be too altruistic.

In the meantime, the money situation worsened. The generous household allowance my father gave my mother had to be tightened, and then tightened again.

I don't remember a single night of my childhood that my father was home for an entire evening, except for the Friday evening in May when he didn't go back to work. He said he wasn't feeling well.

The month of May was dedicated to the Blessed Virgin. The nuns suggested that it would be nice if good Catholic

children, especially the girls, made the sacrifice of going to Mass on Saturday morning. That was why on Saturday, May 6, 1939, I was returning from the seven o'clock Mass when I turned the corner on Tenbroeck Avenue and saw a police car outside our house. My father had died in his sleep.

He was scheduled to go into court on Monday. A judgment had been issued against him for an overdue liquor bill. My mother had begged him to call the supplier, ask for more time, explain that no one was paying him. His answer had been, "Nora, a gentleman pays his bills." He was fifty-four years old.

I'd always been a "Daddy's girl." On Cape Cod, the early settlers called it the "tortience," that special bond which often exists between a father and daughter. My father had been born in Roscommon, Ireland, and came to the United States in 1905 when he was twenty-one. I have the record of his arrival at Ellis Island that states he had five pounds in his pocket. Ten years later he became an American citizen. In those days he had to swear that he was neither an anarchist nor a polygamist and that he renounced his loyalty to George V, king of England.

The time I had with him was all too limited. Looking back, I'm glad that I had severe childhood asthma and frequently missed school. When the attacks came, I'd spend a good part of the night wheezing and gasping for breath, but in the morning the asthma would ease off, and I'd go downstairs to share brunch with him.

A certain scent still reminds me of his shaving lotion. Phrases of songs he sang to me, off-key if my aunt Agnes was

to be believed, still run through my mind. "*Sunday night is my delight . . .* "That's all I can remember. The rest of the words are gone.

My memory of his physical appearance remains vivid, as I see a man just under six feet tall with thinning hair and a strong face. He had a quiet voice. " 'Tis, dear," was the way he would answer my questions in the affirmative. Like the brother and sister who came to the United States within a year or two of him, he did not have a brogue, just a few expressions and a lilt in his voice that was the gift of his Irish ancestry. Years ago I met an elderly cousin in London who had been raised in Ireland. He was the son of my father's oldest sister. "I looked like Luke when I was growing up," he explained. "And as your granddad got older, he would call me Luke. Your dad was his favorite."

My father always intended to go back to Ireland, but he never made it. There was never that much time to get away from the bar and grill.

On Sunday afternoons, he would come home to take us for a drive, and, further proof of our relative early prosperity, we had a summer cottage in Silver Beach Gardens, a small enclave on Long Island Sound at the tip of the east Bronx.

The way to Silver Beach passed St. Raymond's Cemetery. He would point out the flower shop adjacent to the cemetery. It had a small porch with an outdoor table. "And there, my dear," he would remind me, "is the place where the ransom note for the baby was left."

The Crime of the Century. The kidnapping of the Lindbergh baby. The first tangible clue, the ransom note had been placed beneath *that* table.

We did have one memorable outing when I was five years old. My cousin Veronica had decided to become a nun, and we went to visit her in Tarrytown at the convent where she was a postulant.

It was a snowy day, and the convent was at the top of a steep hill. The road was slick with ice, and the car started to slide backwards, weaving from side to side as it meandered with increasing speed down toward the busy road. Joseph and I were in the back seat, my mother in front. As my father frantically tried to regain control of the automobile, Mother cried, "Luke. Luke. Stop the car. Think of the children!"

"God almighty, Nora," he barked. "Do you think this is my idea of driving?"

I remember standing in the backyard with him, shortly before he died, as he pointed to a dirigible floating overhead. It was the *Hindenberg,* and my father explained that it was the new way people would travel long distances. It exploded minutes later in one of the most famous disasters of the twentieth century, and I always claimed that I heard the explosion. But probably it was the sound of it on the radio report that became seared in my mind.

"Sunday night is my delight . . ." The rest of the song is gone. Just as I knew in those first moments as I raced up the stairs, ran down the hall into the bedroom, sank to my knees,

and reached for his hand that Daddy was gone. Three days later, Eddy came down the block, the Good Humor bells jingling. He asked me why I was dressed up. I explained that we had been at my father's funeral.

He was shocked. "If I had known, I wouldn't have rung my bells on this block," he said apologetically.

Ask not for whom the bells toll—or don't toll.

My father had paid Social Security for his employees, but it was six months after his death that the law was changed to include employers. Mother tried to get a job, but she was sent home by the employment agencies.

"We can't get work for college graduates," they told her. "You're fifty-two and haven't held a job in fourteen years. Go home and save your carfare."

That was when she put on her "thinking cap," as she called it, and decided that the solution would be to rent rooms. Once more, I gave up my little room, and we all moved downstairs. The dining room was turned into a bedroom, and a divan was put in the living room.

Mother reasoned that by renting the two big bedrooms for five dollars a week each, and my room for three dollars, we'd make enough to cover the interest on the mortgage and taxes on the house. At that time so many people could no longer afford to amortize their mortgages that the banks had suspended their demand for payments. They didn't want all the houses dumped on them.

Mother didn't drive, and since the car had been sold, she

figured that we might be able to rent the garage for five dollars a month. In the meantime she would stretch the two thousand dollars in insurance money as far as possible.

Joe turned thirteen the week after my father died. He took a newspaper route. Mother began baby-sitting, and so did I. There was a neighbor whose infant I happily minded as I tried to puzzle out the gossip I had heard that the neighbor had been "caught during the change."

Johnnie volunteered to help clean out the garage to get it ready for a potential renter and ended up setting fire to it.

It turned out to be a good fire. We got insurance money for the screens that were stored on the shelves in the back of the garage, along with several carpets and other odds and ends.

Mother never would take a penny that wasn't hers, but she believed passionately in the beauty and value of everything she owned. The results of the fire were shiny new screen doors and windows and some much-appreciated cash, which compensated her for her "good rugs."

She put a discreet sign next to the front door: FURNISHED ROOMS. KITCHEN PRIVILEGES.

The neighbors didn't mind "Furnished Rooms." But "Kitchen Privileges," they hinted, brought down the tone of the neighborhood. Ever obliging, Mother cut the bottom half off the sign, thankful that she hadn't wasted money on a metal sign that would have proved unalterable.

She also put an ad in the *Bronx Home News*.

The next day we waited for the phone to ring.

With my brothers, Joseph and John, on Tenbroeck Avenue, 1933.

Two

The first call came from someone who identified herself as Mrs. Vivian Fields; she requested information on how to get to the house.

On receiving directions, she confirmed that she and her husband would arrive at three o'clock to inspect the room.

Joe and John and I each anticipated our boarders with different emotions. Joe hated change. He wanted everything to be the way it was. He never complained. He was just very quiet.

Johnny was only seven and always had been Joe's shadow. Now more than ever, he looked up to him. Joe was the one who explained to him that when people came to live with us, he couldn't be jumping from the fourth or fifth step to the landing. He'd have to walk quietly up and down the stairs.

I actually was looking forward to our potential paying guests. Without Daddy, the house was too quiet. I missed him

fiercely and hoped that the constant presence of other adults would help to compensate for the void his death had left in our lives.

At five of three, Joe and John and I were standing watch at the living room windows. A car came slowly down the block, stopped two houses away as though the driver was checking house numbers, then started again and parked in front of our house.

We all yelled for Mother, and she hurried to the window in time to see a man and woman get out of the car. "Mary, sit at the piano and play something," she ordered. "It sounds so lovely as you come up the walk."

"I thought you were trying to rent rooms," Joe protested.

I wasn't insulted; I knew, both despite and thanks to several stabs at piano lessons, that I had absolutely no aptitude for anything musical.

Vivian and Eddie Fields were both in their early forties. She was a very pretty woman, whose only lapse was the small vanity of constantly remarking to the world in general that she had just turned thirty-three.

When they told Mother they wanted to rent the big front room and the garage, but they felt five dollars a month for the garage was a little steep for their budget, Mother immediately acquiesced and threw the garage in gratis.

On the way out, Vivian casually remarked that Buck was surely going to enjoy his new home.

"Buck?" Mother asked.

"Our dog."

Mother's face fell. Johnny and I had asthma, and she'd been warned never to bring pets into the house. On the other hand, she didn't want to lose her paying tenants.

"How big is he?" she asked.

Vivian made a kind of cupping gesture with her hands. Her gesture made one think of a tiny poodle or Maltese.

They moved in the next day. If the amount of luggage brought in by our previous brief tenant had awed us, nothing under the sun could have prepared us for the sight of Buck, a wild-eyed boxer we first glimpsed straddling the back seat of their car, his head sticking out one window, his stubby tail arrogantly protruding from the other.

Vivian came in first and suggested that it might be wise if the children waited in the dining room with the doors closed until Buck was safely in their bedroom.

That became our permanent station every morning and evening when Eddie took Buck out for an airing. We watched, our noses glued to the glass panes of the french doors, as Eddie, a slight man, came flying down the stairs, a virtual Peter Pan hanging onto the leash of Buck, who by then was frantic to relieve himself.

A few weeks later, Eddie's wallet slipped out of his pocket. Mother ran after him to return it, but not before she had seen his driver's license in the name of Edward Keener.

Embarrassed, he explained that Ed Fields was his sister's husband. Bill collectors were trying to find him because of the failure of his dealership, and so to avoid being hounded, he was using the alias. Mother of all people understood how it felt to be hounded for payments; she sympathized and kept his secret.

The Fields-Keeners stayed with us for nearly two years, until they got back on their feet. In all that time, Vivian never did turn thirty-four.

We had several single men tenants, and before they moved in, Mother delivered what we called her "palace guard" speech. "Yes," she would tell them, "we are blessed with excellent police protection here. There's Officer Potters to the left, and Officer Ahlis on the right. There's Sergeant Garrigan across the street and directly opposite him . . ." here she paused so the full weight of her pièce de résistance could sink in, ". . . directly opposite him, we have *Inspector* Whelan."

Mother had been going steady with a moving man when she was in her twenties and had somehow caught the virus that is the sine qua non of his profession: she *loved* to move furniture. We all learned to recognize that speculative look in her eyes. "I was thinking if we put the piano at the window and the couch on the stair wall and . . ." No matter how loud and heartfelt our protests, Joe and John and I would find ourselves on the lighter end of the piece to be moved, lifting and hauling as she admonished, "Now don't strain yourself."

The intransigence of our parlor furniture led to the entrapment of one paying guest who was two weeks behind in his rent and was trying to tiptoe out at dawn. Unfortunately for his scheme, we had moved the furniture the night before, and he tripped over a lamp that had been freshly placed on the landing near the bottom of the staircase. Mother rushed out from the dining-room-turned-bedroom to find him sprawled on the floor, his feet entangled in the lamp cord.

She sighed. "If you didn't have the money to pay, all you had to do was tell me," she said, "God knows I can understand that." When he left, he had two dollars pressed in his hand. He claimed he'd been promised a job in New Jersey. It would be nice to say that our departing roomer never forgot the kindness and returned the gift a thousandfold, but unfortunately that was not the case. The guy was a deadbeat.

His spot in my little room was taken over by Herbie Katz, a twenty-one-year-old doctoral candidate who was working for the WPA. He was so skinny that Mother invited him to dinner regularly, which was a pain in the neck for Joe and John and me. We liked Herbie, but he always brought his Victrola to the table and waved his fork to accompany the dirgelike music he favored. If we tried to talk, he raised his other hand to his lips and whispered, "Shhhhhussssh."

Our other memorable paying guest was Madeline Mills, a sixtyish grammar school teacher who valiantly tried to teach me to play the piano. I never got past "Drifting," and I was

much more interested in hearing about Harold, the great love of Miss Mills's life.

Harold had been gassed during World War I. When he returned from overseas, he was in the hospital for a long time while he and Miss Mills prayed that his lungs would heal. Then one day when she visited him, he gave her a single rose and a poem he had written. She recited the poem for me while tears rolled down her cheeks. I forget most of it, but it ended with, "Forgive me if I lay the burden down a little sooner."

Miss Mills had a gentleman friend, Gunther, a reserved and kindly fellow-teacher who was her devoted escort. As I took a break from struggling through the first few pages of John Thompson's piano book for beginners, she confided that at one time she had been engaged to Gunther, but then the husband of the young German woman to whom he had been giving English lessons had named him as the corespondent in their divorce.

"Gunther swore it was a lie, but I broke the engagement, and we just stayed friends," she explained. "That was many years ago."

Her eyes strayed to Harold's picture when she spoke, and I knew that she didn't refuse to marry Gunther because he may have been involved with another woman—it was because she didn't love him enough, and she couldn't stop loving Harold.

I used that plot in a story I wrote that was one of the many

literary efforts of my teenage years. I remember the way the story ended:

> *Happiness is like mercury. Hard to hold, and when we drop it, it shatters into a million pieces. Maybe the bravest of all are those who have the courage to reach for it again.*

Can't you just tell I was born to be a writer?

With Joseph, a photo taken at a family party, circa 1935.

THREE

*W*e all attended St. Francis Xavier Grammar School. Joe graduated in 1940, the year after my father died.

My mother's occupation and hobby, vocation and avocation was motherhood. She loved the three of us fiercely, but there's no question that Joseph was the center of her heart.

It is said that a Jewish mother looks into the cradle and sees a possible Messiah. It's equally true that an Irish mother gazes at her first-born son and sees the Christ child. Joseph was a premature baby, weighing only four pounds when he was born. She fed him with an eyedropper those first months and scarcely left him for an instant. After she died, I found a diary she had kept, and in it she wrote, "I was so afraid he'd slip away. He was such a beautiful baby. The other two had allergies."

Growing up, Joseph justified her pride in him. He won the General Excellence medal all eight years of grammar school,

even though in the eighth grade he missed forty days of school. Six months after Daddy died, Joe cut his heel on the jagged edge of the metal stripping on a door. The infection traveled through his system, and within a week, he was in the hospital in critical condition with osteomyelitis.

Mother was told that an operation to remove his leg at the hip was necessary to save his life. Widowed only a few months, she made the stunning decision not to operate. She wouldn't make a cripple of Joseph, and she knew God wouldn't take him from her.

It was Christmas Eve, my twelfth birthday. The doctors held no hope for Joe's recovery. Mother and John and I carried all his presents to the hospital. His main gift was a hockey stick. "You'll use it next year," she promised him.

Joe needed a lot of blood transfusions, and they literally poured in. Neighbors, relatives, people who only vaguely knew Joe made the trek to Columbia Presbyterian Hospital to offer blood. That Christmas Eve, twenty-year-old Warren Clark, who had just returned from college, was there and rushed to the hospital when he heard Joe was sick.

They were special friends. Joe was such a good ballplayer that when the college guys were home, he was asked to join their impromptu teams. The Clarks lived around the corner from us, and Warren's eight-year-old brother, Ken, was Johnny's best friend.

Warren drove us home that day, and seeing that our Christmas tree was still leaning against the wall in the

foyer, offered to put it up for us. "I'm no St. Joseph," he apologized as he hacked at the trunk, "but maybe I can get it in the stand."

I sat crosslegged on the floor, sorting lights and ornaments and stealing glances at him.

The doctors told Mother there was a new sulfa drug that was being used successfully in the war in Europe. She gave them permission to try it with Joe, and he recovered to the point that when he accepted the General Excellence medal in June, there was no trace of the limp that the doctors had warned might never fully go away.

Blessed with a fine singing voice, Joe was always the star of the annual school play, and he was the captain of the sports teams as well.

Johnny had a good voice too. On the other hand, I was born tone deaf, and while I loved acting, I never did get a speaking part in a school play.

That almost changed when I was in the sixth grade. That year the end-of-the-term school play was based on the legend of Evangeline and Gabriel. The three upper classes all performed in it. There were sixty of us in the sixth grade, and the way Miss Lanning, the music teacher/director, disposed of us was masterful. When Evangeline and Gabriel announce their engagement, Evangeline's mother cries out, "We must invite the villagers to celebrate with us."

That was the cue for the sixth grade to come thudding in from the wings.

And at last I got my speaking part. In rehearsals, I rushed to the front. Center stage. The spotlight fell on me. And I gushed, "Come. Let us dance to the music of this happy day!"

We then lumbered through some kind of group folk dance and within three minutes were off the stage, having satisfied our beaming parents and not having substantially slowed up the progress of the evening.

A speaking part!

I practiced for months.

Was it better to say, "Come. *Let us dance* to the music of this *HAPPY DAY!*"

Or "COME. Let us dance to the MUSIC OF THIS HAPPY DAY!"

Or should I punch every letter of every word? *"COME. LET US DANCE TO THE MUSIC OF THIS HAPPY DAY!"*

I decided on the last version.

The night of the play arrived. I was in a twitter of anticipation but totally without stage fright. I knew I was going to be great.

Then, three minutes before the sixth grade was to go on stage to celebrate the engagement of Gabriel and Evangeline, Sister Mary Laurentia, the principal, came to me, her kindly face troubled.

A girl in the eighth grade was crying her eyes out. She was about to graduate and she had never had a speaking part in one of the plays. Would I consider making a very special sacrifice?

So I never did get to say, "Come. Let us dance to the music of this happy day." Oddly enough, I wasn't upset or unhappy. Even then I thought it was kind of funny.

I guess I'd always realized that it was a dumb line, no matter *how* you delivered it.

My brother Joseph, October 1944.

Four

I graduated from St. Francis a year after Joseph and was awarded a scholarship to Villa Maria Academy, a toney school run by the Congregation de Notre Dame de Montreal. Situated on a former estate on Long Island Sound in the Pelham Bay section of the Bronx, it was a lovely place; my aunts, however, weren't sure I should accept the scholarship.

"She won't be able to keep up with the other girls, Nora," they said, worried, to my mother. "The others will have more clothes and more spending money."

Their warnings fell on deaf ears. I wanted to go to the Villa, and my mother wanted me to go. As she pointed out, there was nothing to worry about. There was a school uniform. I'd be dressed like everyone else.

And so it was—at least to a degree. We hadn't read the fine print saying that uniforms weren't required on the first day of school, so I arrived, the only one in a droopy jumper

and jacket with a long-sleeved blouse, tie, hat and gloves, and oxfords.

It was a hot September day. Everyone else was wearing pretty summer dresses. To compound the error, it was only when we had unpinned the blouse that we realized it required cufflinks. Since there were none in the house, I sat through that first day miserably aware the pins holding the cuffs together were clearly visible.

Collegiate Outfitters had a lock on the business from all the Catholic schools in those days, and my classmates and I were sure that they were a front for Omar the Tent Maker. During the next four years, although I gained fifteen pounds and grew four inches, that uniform was still hanging off me when I wore it on my last day as a senior. You can imagine what a godforsaken waif I must have looked like as a freshman.

Needless to say, as soon as we got over the terror of being brand new freshmen, we began stretching the limits of the dress code. We all hated the clumpy oxfords and would wear penny loafers instead, explaining to the nuns that our oxfords were with the shoemaker being soled or heeled.

You could get away with that for a while, but then the day would come when the homeroom teacher would sternly demand that all the young ladies wearing "bedroom slippers"— the faculty's definition of loafers—were to stand up. A lecture and detention followed, and for a few weeks we'd all come dragging in, wearing oxfords, and then the cycle would begin again.

In those days the nuns were addressed as "Mother." There

were Mother Superior, Mother St. Margaret of the Angels, Mother St. Thomas of Canterbury, Mother St. Patrick of Charity. Of course, they became known more familiarly among us as Soupy, Maggie, Tommy, and Patty. Very *quietly* among us, of course.

When a nun came into the room, we jumped to our feet. "Good morning, young ladies," she would greet us.

As we curtsied, we'd murmur, "Good morning, Reverend Mother."

In those four years there was only one nun who almost all of us thoroughly disliked. She used her tongue like a razorblade, and her goal in life seemed to be to reduce at least one student per class to tears. The fact that she was only in her late twenties still makes it hard for me to fathom why she was so downright mean.

I wonder if any adult—parent or teacher—realizes that young people never forgive or forget being humiliated.

This nun let nothing go unnoticed. Besides being a martinet in the classroom, she would glide past the lunch tables to see if she could spot anyone with an elbow on the table or not sitting up straight. One day she came to our table to challenge a student whose egg salad sandwich had not been cut to her satisfaction. "Young ladies eat only dainty sandwiches," she informed that girl with withering condescension. There was no knife on the table, so she attempted to break the sandwich into sections, and to our infinite delight the egg salad spattered all over her. It made our day.

Another time, when our class filed into chapel, she was kneeling in front of the crucifix, her arms outstretched. There wasn't another nun who wouldn't have immediately dropped her arms when the chapel door opened, but this one wanted to show the depth of her piety. Joan, my closest friend, and I sat next to each other. Talking in chapel could really get you in hot water, but seeing the nun in her pious position, Joan leaned over and whispered, "If I only had a hammer and nails."

All the other nuns were great. In those four years, we received a fine education and a sense of self-worth. It felt good to be a Villa girl. The principal was also the senior-class homeroom teacher and she generously encouraged my writing. Not that I needed much encouragement. I was always writing a short story, including those times when I should have been paying attention in math or science classes. That habit, of course, did not endear me to Mother St. Thomas, the teacher of those subjects.

In fact, forty years after I graduated from the Villa I stopped in for a visit. I found Mother St. Thomas, age ninety, sitting in a wheelchair. She was not eleven feet tall as I had remembered her, but her clear gray eyes were unchanged, and after all those years she still had me pegged.

"Miss Higgins, you were a dreadful math student," she said severely.

I swept into a curtsey. "God bless your memory, Reverend Mother."

*   *   *

My first attempt to sell a short story came when I was sixteen. Having studied the market, I decided that everything *True Confessions* magazine published was so bad that they might even accept something from me. However, "Give Love a Chance" and "I, with My Guilt" came back by return mail, so I decided I needed a little more life experience before I attacked the publishing world again.

At the same time, I decided that babysitting didn't pay enough and began to work three afternoons after school and weekends as a switchboard operator at the old Shelton Hotel on Forty-ninth Street and Lexington Avenue in Manhattan. For an aspiring writer, it was an absolutely fantastic job. I quickly mastered the ability to listen in on conversations undetected. Usually undetected, that is.

The way it worked was that if my switchboard wasn't busy with incoming or outgoing calls, I would pull the master cord partly out of the socket. That meant I could open the key without the telltale clicking sound that alerted people to the fact that a busybody operator was enjoying their conversation.

My favorite eavesdropee was Ginger Bates, a lady of easy virtue who was a permanent resident of the Shelton. I loved listening to her chat with her various and plentiful admirers. One day I obviously had not pulled out the master switch far enough because she suddenly told her caller, "Don't say another word. That damn operator is listening in."

"I am not," I said indignantly, then in horror disconnected

the call before it could be traced to my board. A moment later, the chief operator bellowed, "Who just had Ginger Bates?"

The picture of innocence, I was busy responding to an incoming call. "Hotel Shelton, good afternoon."

Knowing it was useless, the chief operator did not pursue her search for the culprit. "For God's sake, girls, if you're going to listen in, at least be smart about it," she snapped.

I was very careful when I listened in on Tennessee Williams, that would-be playwright with the crazy name, as the senior operators described him. At that time he had the cheapest room in the hotel—thirty dollars a month, less than a dollar a day, as one of them pointed out.

But I didn't hear anything that fascinated me. Years later, when a mutual friend gave Williams a copy of the manuscript for *Where Are the Children?*, which had just been sold to Simon & Schuster, his comment was, "I have a lot of friends who can write better than that," so I guess I didn't fascinate him either. We'll call it a draw.

On the days I worked at the Shelton, I would take the bus to the train and ride to downtown Manhattan. If I made good time, I'd scurry over to Fifth Avenue and slowly walk down the ten blocks from Fifty-ninth to Forty-ninth Street, windowshopping, choosing the clothes I would buy when I was a successful writer. I'd linger at Bergdorf Goodman, then Tailored Woman, and Bonwit Teller and DePinna and Saks, carefully selecting my future wardrobe.

Now, on the first Tuesday of every month, I have dinner

with a dozen fellow mystery-suspense writers in a restaurant on Forty-ninth Street. From our private, second-floor dining room, I can look across the street at the employees' entrance of the Shelton and, directly overhead, the windows of the switchboard room where I toiled all those afternoons and weekends. It doesn't seem that long ago.

By the time I was completing my sophomore year at the Villa, our tenants the Fields-Keeners had departed. Miss Mills had found an apartment near her school. The war economy had opened new jobs, and Herbie Katz, too nearsighted to pass the army physical, was working in a defense factory on Long Island. He never did come back to collect all the funeral music he had played for us so often. I wonder if by then he was sick of it, too.

In spite of all our concerted efforts, the roomers who came and went, my work at the Shelton, Mother's baby-sitting jobs and Joe's newspaper route, we couldn't keep up the overhead on Tenbroeck Avenue, and finally we lost the house. Mother was urged to take Joseph out of school and put him to work, but she refused. "Education is more important than any house," she said firmly. "Joseph will get his diploma."

I have not been in the Tenbroeck Avenue house since, but it is still fresh in my mind. I can clearly see the soft ivory walls of the living room, the carpet with the center design that made a perfect goal when we shot marbles. The Horace Waters piano is in place again near the staircase. I can feel the

comfort of the overstuffed velour chairs by the fireplace, where Joe and I companionably sprawled side by side with our books. Again I stand on the landing on the staircase where I staged the plays I wrote, and where little Johnny would patiently recite his lines. I am propped up in bed in my little room, hearing my Mother calling, "Mary, is the light off?"

"Yes," I honestly answer—but I am reading the book by the streetlight that conveniently streams onto my pillow.

Our next stop was a three-room apartment near the trolley line, and into it Mother moved the full contents of the six rooms we'd had formerly, sure that someday our fortunes would change and we'd get our house back. We never did, though, and whenever she returned from visiting the old neighborhood, her eyes would shine with unshed tears as she remarked how beautifully her roses had grown.

Joe turned eighteen, graduated from high school in 1944, and promptly enlisted in the navy.

The war had broken out three years earlier, and even though the Villa was a small school, with increasing frequency morning prayers began with the announcement, "We will pray for the repose of the soul of Anita's brother, John . . . of Mother St. Margaret's nephew, Danny . . ." And then it was my turn: "We will pray for the repose of the soul of Mary Higgins's brother, Joseph."

Mother could have claimed Joe as her sole support and kept him out of service. Instead she let him enlist in the navy with his friends. Six months later, she took the only long trip

of her life, a plane ride to California to be at Joe's deathbed in the Long Beach Naval Hospital. While in training school, he had contracted spinal meningitis. To the people who fumbled for words of sympathy, she said, "It is God's will. I couldn't let Joseph go when he was sick the other time, but now God wants him even more than I do."

That June when I graduated from the Villa, she threw a party for me where she allowed no hint of sadness. It was my day, and nothing was going to spoil it. Johnny graduated from grammar school a few weeks later and he, too, had all the aunts and uncles and cousins and friends there to celebrate. She bought a black-and-white print dress to wear to both occasions. She felt her black mourning dress was out of place those two days.

We three siblings had been so close, Joseph, Mary, and John. J.M.J. Joe's death multiplied a thousand times the sense of loss that I'd felt since that May morning five years earlier when I came home to the news that "Daddy's dead."

That sense of loss had a lot to do with my deciding to go to secretarial school rather than college. I wanted to grow up. I wanted to earn money. I wanted to marry young and have children. As I had welcomed our paying guests to help fill the void in our house left by my father, now I was looking forward to that future family, the husband who at the end of the day would turn his key in the lock and call, "I'm home," the grandchildren who would fill my mother's arms.

I came across a fragment of a poem I wrote that first year

after Joe died: "I was dressed in garments thin, I was the outsider looking in . . ."

Dreadful poetry, but I remember the moment I wrote it. I was on my way home one evening from the job at the Shelton. It was a winter night and terribly cold on the platform as I got off the train and hurried down the steps and through the cavernous station to wait, shivering, for the trolley. Other people had fathers waiting to pick them up and family dinners on the table at home, with everyone together. I wanted to recreate that kind of world for us.

Looking back, I could easily have gotten a scholarship to several colleges but instead elected to accept the partial scholarship offered by Wood Secretarial School. It would only cost me two hundred and fifty dollars rather than four hundred for the one-year term. When I got there and compared notes with the other students, we could find only one girl who was paying the full four hundred. All the rest of us had received "partial scholarships."

A year later, now equipped with reasonably good office skills, I was given a list of places to go for job interviews. The first one was a dingy office way downtown where they manufactured window shades. I was offered the job immediately, thirty-five dollars a week, two weeks vacation. "You'll love it here, Miss Higgins. You'd be surprised how interesting the window-shade business can be. Something new comes up every minute!"

Not wanting to hurt the feelings of the enthusiastic office manager, I accepted the job and went onto the next interview, which was with a tool-and-dye manufacturer. Once again I was offered the job, and for exactly the same money. Once again, not wanting to hurt anyone's feelings, I accepted it.

The third stop was at Remington Rand, the premium typewriter–office equipment producer. But this situation was different. The company had its own in-house advertising agency, and the minute I got off the elevator at the eleventh floor, I knew that this was where I wanted to be. Except for the private corner office of the Advertising Manager, the whole floor was open, divided into waist-high cubicles. I could see copywriters pounding their typewriters, artists sketching, runners hurrying to the area marked PRODUCTION. There was a sense of electricity in the air, and I wanted to be part of it.

The job was secretary to the creative director, who was second in command of the department. Sterling Jessup Hiles was a tall, lean man whose glasses seemed to be part of his face. I liked him immediately. I liked the way he talked to the people who ran in to interrupt him during our interview: "Jess, sorry to butt in, but I need a fast okay on this change . . ."

"Jess, will you take a quick look at this caption . . ."

"I'm sorry, Miss Higgins," he would apologize as he attended to the interruptions. As I observed his unflappable, easygoing manner, I knew that I desperately wanted that job.

Unlike my earlier experiences that day, I was not hired on the spot. "This is a pretty responsible job, Miss Higgins," he said. "I'm afraid eighteen is a bit young for it."

I earnestly assured him I could handle it but left worrying about the other candidates he would be interviewing. I was to call him the next day at three o'clock.

I left the Remington Rand offices knowing that whether I got the job or not, I didn't want to be mesmerized by how interesting the window-shade business could be, nor did I want to increase my knowledge of the tool-and-die industry. I called and begged off from those opportunities for gainful employment.

The next twenty-four hours passed with agonizing slowness. Finally it was three o'clock on the following day, and with fervent prayers to all my favorite saints, I made the call.

The following Monday, I reported to work at Remington Rand. Even the starting salary was better than my other two job offers: $37.50 a week.

I was on my way in the business world.

As Sterling Hiles's secretary, I sat in on all the creative meetings. I didn't realize it, but I was getting a tutorial in advertising and promotion. I was learning why this ad campaign worked and why another was less successful, why one slogan caught on and another one did not, why this caption didn't cut the mustard while another one sold thousands of typewriters or adding machines.

At night I began taking courses at the Advertising Club and began to get assignments to write small items of catalog copy.

When I'd been two years at Remington, John William Kean the Ninth, a thirty-year-old copywriter, asked me to join him for a drink after work. Of average height with dark hair, a mustache, and a deep, knowing chuckle, he seemed to me to be the epitome of worldliness.

His last job had been as an attaché at the American Embassy in Greece. Since I passionately longed to travel and considered anyone who had made it out of the tristate area a seasoned explorer, Jack's former employment enhanced his man-about-town image for me.

Remington Rand was on the corner of Twenty-third Street and Fourth Avenue. We met at the front door and walked from there to Eddie's Aurora, a small Italian restaurant in Greenwich Village. Its backroom was the hangout of Jack's arty friends.

There I met Dorothea, a widow in her early thirties, still deeply mourning the husband who had died in service, and Joe Carroll, her patient and steadfast admirer. Also in the group were a number of struggling artists and actors, a few of the people from Jack's diplomatic corps days, and some unpublished writers.

I was dazzled by their worldliness, and Jack and I started to go there several times a week. The regulars all had fine voices, and toward the end of the evening, when they were

quite mellow, they would begin to sing. Arias from operas, George Gershwin melodies, hit songs of the day. They always wound up the evening with a spirited rendition of "Waltzing Matilda."

Jack disdained my order of "rye and ginger ale, please," and ordered me my first scotch. Halfway through each evening, a flower lady who must have been eighty years old came in and went from table to table selling gardenias for fifty cents. He always bought one and pinned it on my shoulder with elaborate courtliness.

My mother, although she hadn't laid eyes on him, worried about my dating Jack. She thought that "from the sound of him" he was too sophisticated for me. And he wasn't Catholic. That was a huge no-no.

We dated on and off for about six months; then I invited him to a family party. The old girls looked him over. One of them called me aside. "Take a look, dear," she whispered. "He has small feet, and you know, dear, small feet, small understanding."

The others nodded solemnly, agreeing that Jack was not the right person for me. I am sure they must have made a flying novena to St. Jude to break up the budding romance because the next week Jack called me at home, slightly in his cups, to announce happily that he'd made up with his old girlfriend. Since he had never taken her picture out of his wallet, I wasn't all that surprised.

Actually he didn't call me at home. We didn't have a tele-

phone, and even though we had applied for one now that I was working, we were on a long waiting list for installation. Alice, who had the candy store around the corner liked me and agreed that if it didn't happen too often, I could get a call there. Jack was one of the few who had the number, so I had to swallow my pride and listen to his ecstatic ramblings while standing in the phone booth of a candy store.

Not wanting to be considered the dumpee, I told him it was fine with me if we stopped seeing each other and added, "There's someone I've always liked. His name is Warren Clark. He's twenty-nine and always thought of me as a kid, but now I understand he's been asking about me. I see him every week in church at the 12:15 Mass."

That last part at least was true. I did see Warren Clark at the 12:15 Mass, but any attraction was on my part, not his. Warren attended Mass with his mother and two brothers. The younger one, Ken, was Johnny's best friend. Mrs. Clark was a stately, elegant woman; Allan, the middle brother, was always crisply groomed; Ken looked perpetually sleepy; and Warren, whom I later learned always got out of bed at the last minute, was often adjusting his tie.

I made it my business to greet Mrs. Clark every Sunday after Mass, and she said in passing to my brother that I was a very attractive girl. Then one Sunday she asked John, "Didn't I hear that your sister is engaged to be married?"

"Who'd marry your sister?" Warren asked Johnny, laughing. John and Ken were inseparable, and my brother spent a

great deal of time in the Clark home. He was always quoting Warren, saying how funny he was and how the girls were calling him all the time.

John couldn't wait to relay the conversation that related to me. He didn't need to tell me that Warren was joking, but I made a silent vow: You'll want to marry me someday, pal. Just wait and see.

I was philosophic about my breakup with Jack Kean. I knew he wasn't right for me. In my diary I wrote: "Jack, you will always remind me of being twenty. The taste of scotch. The scent of a gardenia. And the sound of 'Waltzing Matilda.'"

My best friend at Remington was Joan Murchison. Blond and very pretty, she was a copywriter for the electric shaver division and at the time was dating Dennis James, who was a rising star in the infant television industry.

He broadcast the immensely popular wrestling matches, and had his own daytime series as well, entitled, God help us, *Okay, Mother.* He was also the host of a Sunday evening talent show, *Chance of a Lifetime.*

Joan and he broke up right at the time Jack and I went kaput, so we tried to get the word around the company that we were eminently available for dates. But you can't very well wear a sign to that effect, so many evenings we'd have a Coke or a glass of wine together, lamenting our dateless state. Then

she'd go to the Barbizon Hotel for Women where she lived, and I'd take the subway home to the Bronx.

I liked my job, but I was becoming increasingly restless. I was being given catalog copy to write, and I was also asked to model for some of the company brochures. Incidentally, I was in good company there. The future actress Grace Kelly was also picking up extra money modeling for those catalogs, and soon-to-be novelist Joe Heller was a junior copywriter.

I didn't really want to write catalog copy, though. I wanted to be a short-story writer. I began to study the market, the slicks as the popular women's magazines of the day were called: *Ladies' Home Journal, McCall's, Woman's Home Companion, Redbook, Family Circle, Woman's Day, Collier's.* And of course there was the crème de la crème of popular fiction, *The Saturday Evening Post.* I longed to be one of the contributors to any of those magazines. I started attempting to write, but knew that what I was doing wasn't on target. Just as when I received my rejections from *True Confessions,* I knew I needed to know more about life and the world around me.

Then one afternoon Joan told me she was going to have a glass of wine with a friend who was a Pan American Airlines flight hostess, and she asked if I wanted to join them.

"God knows I have nothing else to do," I assured her. We met Katie Miles in a small hotel on Madison Avenue and Twenty-eighth Street. She was late, but when she arrived, she stopped traffic.

Katie was a drop-dead beautiful girl in her midtwenties. She had red hair, violet eyes, and a porcelain complexion. Slender and tall, she sashayed across the room, and every eye followed her. She was wearing her Pan Am uniform, which I came to learn was absolutely forbidden. No stewardess *ever*— repeat *ever*—was to appear in a cocktail lounge in her uniform.

No matter. Katie always broke the rules.

She spotted us, headed for our table, tossed off her overseas cap, and collapsed onto the banquette. "God, it was beastly hot in Calcutta," she said, sighing deeply.

Those seven words changed my life.

FIVE

The next morning, Joan and I called in sick to Remington Rand and scurried over to Pan Am's office near La-Guardia Airport to apply for jobs. The requirements in those days would bring on a class-action bias suit now. You had to be between twenty-one and twenty-six years of age, between five-two and five-seven in height, and your weight had to be commensurate with height. You couldn't wear glasses. You had to be pretty. You had to have an outgoing personality. You had to have a college education or the kind of job experience that would have made you at ease in dealing with the public. And you had to speak a foreign language.

I had just turned twenty-one. Joan was twenty-eight, but of course she put a doctored birthdate on her résumé. I didn't have a college degree, but the interviewer told me that my experience as secretary to an advertising executive would be sufficient.

We both had a near heart attack when we learned about the foreign language requirement. Joan had had a little French in college, and after four years at Villa Maria, thanks to the Congregation de Notre Dame de Montreal, I could pray in French a lot better than I could converse in it.

The interviewer said we'd be called in for further meetings, but in the meantime we were cautioned, "Girls, bone up on your French."

There was a French expatriate living in the Barbizon for Women, so we paid her a dollar an hour to bat the breeze with us, suggesting she concentrate on such items as "Fasten your seatbelt" and "*La toilette est ici.*" We also ate at restaurants neither one of us could really afford in an effort to familiarize ourselves with French haute cuisine. That money was wasted. The frozen meals served on airlines in 1949 did not require a working knowledge of *any* cuisine. "Try to get it down," would have been sufficient linguistic skill for us to master when it came to mealtime.

We had been asked to submit our birth certificates. It took several copies of Joan's before we successfully altered the year of her birth and made her twenty-six instead of twenty-eight.

Pan Am had three divisions: Atlantic, Pacific, and South American. The Atlantic division encompassed Europe, Africa, and Asia, linking with the Pacific division in Calcutta. We were being considered for the Atlantic Division, for which LaGuardia Airport was the base. Idlewild, now Kennedy International, and now one of the most important air-

ports in the world, was at the time "that mudhole in the middle of the potato fields of Long Island."

Joan and I passed the second interview.

Mother was torn. On the one hand, she was thrilled at the idea of being able to tell everyone that her daughter was a Pan American stewardess. On the other hand, she was terrified that something might go wrong with the plane. An added consideration was the fact that I already had a secure job. Mr. Hiles liked me; suppose the new job didn't work out. Not to mention that I was making fifty-five dollars a week now and Pan American would only pay fifty.

But she was fair. She did accept the rationale that since I'd only just turned twenty-one, I shouldn't yet have to worry about clinging to security. Plus there was a final reason for her to hope along with me that Pan Am would hire me. At heart Mother was adventuresome. During the summer, on her own, she would take one-day outings on a Hudson Day Liner or a bus to the mountains or the shore. She also would often take the train to visit her sister in Rockaway, and there she'd blissfully stroll along the boardwalk. She loved the look and smell of the ocean, a love I inherited.

Support also came from other quarters. Now seventeen and a senior in high school, my younger brother John thought Pan Am was a great idea. Over six feet tall and still growing, blessed with Irish good looks, twinkling blue eyes, and dark brown hair, skinny as God made them, he was a good dancer and a lot of fun. By then Mother and I were the only two who

called him John or Johnny. Everyone else called him Luke. The name my father had given to both his sons only as a middle name, for fear they would find it too Irish, had become the name by which they chose to be called.

Finally Joan and I were down to one final interview. Frantically we went over the departure speech we might be asked to give. "*Bonjour, Messieurs et Mesdames. Je m'appelle Marie Higgins . . .*" We practiced being fluent with such vital phrases as "Would you care to have a Chiclet?"

In those days the hostess passed out chewing gum before departure and landing. The act of chewing helped passengers to equalize the change in air pressure in their ears as the plane took off and landed.

The day came for us to take the French test; when it was finished, though nervous, we decided that we'd done okay. M. Raviol, who had given us the test, kept smiling and nodding as we answered the few simple questions he slowly and carefully asked us "*en français.*"

Two days later we got the call: "Quit your jobs, girls. You are Pan American stewardesses."

I really hated to break the news to Mr. Hiles; he had been so nice to me. But it had to be done. His first stunned reaction was, "But I have just finished teaching you how to spell." Then he sighed and became philosophical: "My theory, which you have just proven, is that a good secretary lasts for three years. Then she gets a better job or gets married."

With my mother and brother John, 1945.

He and his wife invited me to dinner the evening of my last day at Remington Rand. "Bring a date," he urged.

I didn't know whom to invite. I had gone out occasionally with a couple of other guys in the company after Jack, but I wasn't interested in any of them—and to be perfectly honest, they weren't interested in me.

On the other hand, I reasoned, might this not be the time to make a move to catch Warren Clark's eye?

My mother had undergone some minor surgery a few months earlier, and Mrs. Clark had invited John to dinner while Mother was in the hospital, telling him to be sure to bring his sister as well.

The dinner went splendidly. I thought I was being particularly charming, including eating the pistachio ice cream that Warren had brought, but which only he liked. But then, after coffee, Allan, the middle Clark brother who had just become engaged, got up to go to his fiancée's home. John and Ken disappeared to meet their friends, leaving only Mrs. Clark, Warren, and me at the table.

Then to my dismay, Warren stood up. "I'm on my way," he announced cheerfully.

"But, Warren, we have a young lady here, a guest," Mrs. Clark protested.

"Mother," he said, "there is another young lady residing in Parkchester, who at this moment is watching at the window, pining for her prince."

"Warren, you can't mean that little blond girl!"

"Mother, you don't seem to realize. She's built like a brick . . ."

"Warren!"

"A brick establishment, Mother," he said innocently. "Nice to have seen you, Mary."

Not exactly encouraging, I reasoned, but still, why not invite him to the farewell dinner? So he might refuse; I'll be away a lot. I won't have to bump into him at church.

It took all my courage, but I made the call, half hoping he wouldn't be home. But he was.

I chatted with him for a moment, telling him I was about to become a Pan Am stewardess.

He congratulated me.

"I think it's going to be really fascinating," I stammered, playing for time.

"I guess it will be, Mary. Good luck."

There was a good-bye edge of finality in his voice.

"My boss and his wife want to take me to dinner on Friday night. Would you like to join us?"

"This Friday night. Oh, I'm sorry, Mary, I've got something on."

"No, a week from Friday night," I told him.

He couldn't think of a reason to refuse again.

When we hung up, we had a date for dinner.

My cousin Al Hayward was Warren's closest friend. Later I learned that Warren joked to him that he was robbing the cradle, taking out Al's kid cousin.

He met the Hileses and me at the Pennsylvania Hotel. We went to dinner at Charles, then a popular restaurant in Greenwich Village. At 10:30, the Hileses left to catch their train home, and Warren suggested a nightcap at Ernie's Three Ring Circus, an after-dinner spot nearby.

When we were seated there, he ordered both of us a drink. A comedian came on. His material was pretty raunchy and sailed over my head, but hoping not to look stupid, I took my cues from the people at the other tables, and laughed along with them.

Warren had begun writing something on a paper napkin. He looked up at me. "Don't laugh," he said. "You don't understand what he's saying, and anyhow, it isn't funny."

He continued to write, and I could see that he was jotting down names. I asked him who they were.

"The people I'll have at the wedding," he told me. "Fly for a year. Get it out of your system. I'll take my mother to drive-in movies when you're away. We'll get married at Christmas. People are more generous then."

I stared at him.

"Don't go girly and cute," he said. "You know we're going to get married."

I *did* know it. I'd never been more certain of anything in my life.

Six

*T*he following Monday, Joan and I reported to La-Guardia Airport to begin our three-week training course. Flight school in 1949 was held on folding chairs in an empty hangar. Two senior pursers were the instructors.

There were eighteen of us in the group. We were invited to stand up, give our names, and tell where we were from and what we had been doing before we joined Pan Am.

All the minispeeches were routine until a Southern girl with flashing eyes stood up. "Ah'm Bonnie Lee Harding," she announced. "And Ah worked for American Airlines and Ah got fired."

We waited.

"A passenger put a bag that must'ah weighed a ton on the overhead rack," Bonnie Lee explained, her tone heating up at the memory, "and Ah said to him in ma nicest Southern belle manner, 'Excuse me, sir, but Ah'll have ta ask you to take that

bag down and put it under your seat.'" In those days the airplane's overhead luggage racks consisted of loose hanging bins made of rope, and I had heard that during turbulence heavy objects often came tumbling down into the aisles.

"He refused in a very ungentlemanly, brusque way. Ah asked him again. And he refused and told me that he'd just flown on Eastern Airlines and he'd put that same bag overhead on the rack, and it was just fine with everyone.

"Well we had to secure the cabin, and Ah knew the Captain was probably all set to get mad at me for delaying him, and Ah'm afraid Ah lost my temper. *'Eastern!'* Ah said, *'Captain Eddy's Flying Circus!* You're lucky you didn't have a cow up there over your seat, Mister.'" Bonnie Lee sighed. "Unfortunately, ma passenger was a top executive with Cooks Tours and had just given American tons of business, so Ah got fired. And now Ah'm happy to be with all of you."

Some class members looked bewildered. Joan and I felt very much in-the-know. Our stewardess friend Katie Miles had filled us in on the nicknames of the airlines. Eastern, founded and owned by Captain Eddie Rickenbacker, had a reputation for carrying a lot of live animals, which was why it was known as "Captain Eddie's Flying Circus." Pan Am was "Pandemonium World Scareways." TWA was "Teeney Weeney Airlines" or "Try Walking Across." Air France was "Air Chance." Sabena was "Such a Bitter Experience Never Again."

After we'd all been properly introduced, the purser asked

As a flight attendant for Pan Am, I became involved in a media event when I walked an orphaned child from England down the steps from the plane to meet her new adoptive mother.

anyone who had been given the French conversation test by Monsieur Raviol to raise her hand. Joan and I were the only two. "You'll have to take the test over with Phil Parrott," we were told. "We just realized that Monsieur Raviol is only qualified to give the Portuguese test." Joan and I looked at each other in horror. No wonder Monsieur Raviol had asked such simple questions and had such a dreamy look. He knew less French than we did.

There was one obvious solution to the problem: avoidance. I spent the next year ducking Phil Parrott, and Joan spent seven years ducking him.

In the three weeks of training, we learned basic first aid, including how to deliver a baby—a not uncommon possibility at that time, we were warned. War brides were still arriving from Europe, their servicemen husbands' tours of duty now over. Travel agents weren't supposed to sell tickets to anyone who was more than six months pregnant, but that rule was most often honored by its violation. I was to have a number of *enciénte* ladies on my flights whom I nervously anticipated would be visited by the stork while still above the clouds. Fortunately, they all made it to terra firma.

We were told that there was always the possibility of a crash landing at sea. "It's called 'ditching,' " the instructor said matter-of-factly. We learned emergency procedures. "Just remember, girls, water is harder than concrete. But if you get lucky and the plane doesn't break up on contact, it will float anywhere from three minutes to three days. Assume you've

got three minutes. Grab the raft. It's on the wall between the two lavatories. Be sure you have the survival equipment. Open the emergency exit over the wing. Inflate the raft outside the plane. Then . . . and now listen hard . . ." Here the instructor paused for dramatic effect: "Give a mighty sweep of your arm and shout 'Follow me!' "

Then he explained the reason we were to lead the charge to escape: "You people will know how to use the radio to send Mayday signals, as well as how to help possible survivors."

We practiced preparing and serving meals on a plane parked in another hangar. Astonishingly, during the entire training period, we never went up on a test flight. My only prior experience off the ground had come two years earlier, in a one-engine, open-cockpit, two-seater plane piloted by a former air force pilot I had met at my cousin's wedding. He was trying to start his own feeder airline in Far Rockaway. He headed the plane over the Atlantic, then on the intercom told me to put my hand on the stick. When I did, he said, "You're flying the plane, Mary."

I knew no one would be dopey enough to let me take over the controls and said so. "See that stick in front of you? If you don't believe me, move it to the left or right," he urged. I laughed, twisted it all the way to the right, and we came close to flying upside down. "Let go," he bellowed, "let go." As that tiny plane zoomed over the breakers, I fell in love with flight. The pilot, however, was someone I never saw again.

The three weeks training ended, and, bursting with pride,

Joan and I put on our uniforms for the graduation ceremony at which we were handed our wings. My hair was long then, and I wore it in a chignon. It was a very strict rule with the airline that hair was not permitted to touch the collar and, as at the Villa, white gloves were de rigueur.

During the training session, Warren came to see me every evening. Whenever I'd dated before I met him, I'd been secretly unhappy about my family's tiny apartment over the tailor shop. I'd longed to be in our house again, with the big tree that shaded my little room and Mother's roses and hydrangeas in the garden. But Warren couldn't have cared less. He and my mother became fast and devoted friends. She was an ardent Democrat. He was a Republican. The one thing she never forgave him was the fact that, when for the first time I was eligible to vote, he took me to register and "turned me into a Republican." To my mother, it was a sin almost on a par with marrying outside the faith.

After the graduation ceremony, Joan and I went home to await a call from scheduling. Mine came the next day. I was on standby Sunday, which meant I had to be ready to leave for the airport instantly if needed, plus I was scheduled to fly to London on Monday.

At the time, Pan Am had one daily flight to London. It left at four o'clock in the afternoon and landed at Gander, Newfoundland, at eight o'clock, where there was a crew change. It took eleven more hours to fly on to London, and that was considered too much flight time for one crew to handle.

In Gander we slept in barracks, and, to pass the time, went bowling at a place where the lanes were so warped that I got a strike even though my ball went into the alley. The plane we flew was a four-engine, propeller Constellation. It had fifteen rows of seats, two on each side of a center aisle, for a total of sixty passengers, with an extra last double seat on one side for the purser and stewardess.

The flight deck crew consisted of a Captain, First Officer, Navigator, Engineer, Radio Operator, and sometimes an extra pilot. The two cabin personnel were a purser and steward or stewardess. If the purser was male, it was always a stewardess who worked with him. If the purser was female, the reverse was true. The idea was that in the event of a crash/ditching there should be one set of muscles who could physically lift or haul people onto the ground or sea.

On my first flight, I had four infants on board who were going to meet their English grandparents. We'd no sooner set foot on the plane than one young mother attempted to hand me her two-month-old pride and joy. "Baby will have his bottle now," she said sweetly.

I had to gently disabuse her of the notion that the flight hostess was a full-time, on-board nanny, but other than that it was, praise heaven, an uneventful trip, both from New York to Gander, and then Gander to London.

Wednesday afternoon we arrived in Heathrow Airport. I simply could not believe that I was really there, abroad, in England. In the crew bus on the way to the hotel, I sat awestruck,

my face pressed against the window. My first vivid impression was of the number of locations we passed that displayed the sign BOMB PARK. It was now 1949, and the rubble from the war had been cleared, but those empty spaces brought home to me how severely England had suffered during World War II.

We settled in at the Green Park Hotel on Half Moon Street and went down to dinner. The guys told me to be sure to order the roast beef.

I love roast beef and cheerfully obeyed. The waitress's expression became distressed. "Oh, love," she said with a sigh, "I'm so sorry, but . . . *the roast beef's finished.*" The six crew members I was sitting with chimed in to finish the sentence with her, then explained. In post-war London there was an acute shortage of beef, but the Brits did not want to see it disappear from the menu. So it was always listed, and when someone not in the know requested it, the same stock answer was given in restaurants all over England: "Oh, love, I'm sorry, but the roast beef's finished."

It was a gorgeous evening, and after dinner, I eagerly suggested that we all go for a walk. As one, they protested, "Honey, you've walked across the Atlantic. Forget it. We'll take you sightseeing tomorrow. Instead we'll buy you a drink to celebrate your first night in London."

"If you guys think I'm going to sit inside on my first night in London, you're mistaken! No thanks. I'm going out."

I strolled down Half Moon Street to where it terminated

at Green Park, across the road. Feeling as though I were living a dream, I tried to get my bearings. Now let's see, I thought, looking to the right. Trafalgar Square is that way.

A song lyric ran through my head: "A nightingale sang in Barclay Square."

I had carefully studied the guide books. And the palace is just beyond the park, I told myself.

Another song began running through my mind: "I'm going to London to see the queen." And . . .

Suddenly I felt a tap on my shoulder. Startled, I spun around. A thirtyish lady wearing a ton of makeup, a raunchy fur, a hat squashed on a tangled mess of curls, said apologetically, "Beg your pardon, love, but this is my corner."

Welcome to London! I rushed back to the hotel and had a nightcap with the guys.

December 26, 1949. My wedding to Warren Clark, held in the school auditorium because our little church had burned down.

SEVEN

$\mathcal{E}$urope, Africa, Asia. If my mother had been in charge of scheduling, I couldn't have done better with the assignments I got. Nineteen forty-nine was a wonderful time to see the world, just as everything was about to change. My other world was changing, too.

Warren's brother Allan was getting married on June 25 to June Mary Callow, who had been one year ahead of me at St. Francis Xavier. "We won't rain on their parade," Warren told me. He was turning thirty on July 19, and his mother was planning a big party for him. "I'll give you your ring for my birthday, which shows how nice I am. We'll announce our engagement at the party." First, though, we did tell our plans to my mother and Mrs. Clark. Both were delighted, if startled. Of course, our friends began to speculate about us. However, my cousin Al Hayward, who was Warren's best friend, was worried. At the wedding in June, he pulled me aside. "Mary,"

he said, "I don't want you to get hurt. Warren never sticks with any girl for long, so even though I can see he's giving you a big rush, I can promise you it won't last."

"I'll keep that in mind," I promised him solemnly. What I didn't tell my cousin was that Warren and I had selected the setting for my engagement ring the previous evening.

Mother and I began shopping for wedding gowns. I loved the first one I saw—totally traditional, ivory satin with Chantilly lace. But the instincts of the bridal buyer she had been didn't allow my mother to make a choice without comparison shopping. In the end, at Arnold Constable on Fifth Avenue, we bought the first one I had seen and loved. In the interim, however, there wasn't a store in Manhattan or a bridal shop in the tristate area that wasn't given the opportunity to trot out every gown in their stockrooms.

As a wedding present, Mrs. Clark gave us a DeSoto Coupe and a check for five thousand dollars. A couple of months before the wedding, she took me shopping for furniture. "He doesn't know a thing about it, Mary," she said. "We'll make the choice." When we were finished, Warren almost fainted to see that most of the five thousand dollars had disappeared, but Mrs. Clark was right to encourage me to buy good quality. I still have most of that furniture. The car arrived early, and we had it by the end of the summer, well before the wedding. After all the years of buses and trolley cars, it was heaven to find that DeSoto parked in front of the tailor shop when Warr picked me up.

Because back then it took so many flight hours to travel to long destinations, a trip to India took three weeks, a trip to Johannesburg a full month. En route to India, we'd stop for a couple of days in London, then in Damascus, Karachi, and New Delhi, and then we'd stay maybe a week in Calcutta before we started back.

Warren would write to me, and I'd find his letters waiting at various stops. He signed all of them "Warren-you-know-better-than-that." I know it sounds quaint to most people, given today's climate, but in 1949, a well-bred Irish Catholic girl simply did not "fool around," even with her fiancé. An arm around the shoulder, holding hands, a chaste kiss—that was the way it was. And even when they made a pass, the men respected their dates or fiancées for toeing that line. As a result, at the end of the evening, in between kisses goodnight, I would be hissing, "Warren, you know better than that."

Mother, who told me it was her duty to my dead father to see that I came through the dating years unscathed, had guarded me with the vigilance of St. George slaying the dragon. Whenever I would come home with a date, she'd be leaning out the window, dangling dangerously between earth and heaven. "Is that you, Mary?" she'd call.

No, it's Gunga Din, I'd think, but her method worked. No one ever got fresh with me with that alert sentry hovering twenty feet above. All that changed, of course, when Warren and I started going out together. Mother retired, blissful in the knowledge that I was dating Mrs. Clark's son. When I

pointed out that dating Mrs. Clark's son was not precisely the same as dating Mrs. Clark, the reference sailed over her head.

I began shopping for my trousseau—very limited shopping, I might add. But one of the items I selected was a sheer black nightgown. I showed it to Warren, and he managed to read the newspaper through it. My mother was horrified and called me aside. "Mary, you wouldn't put that thing on and wear it in front of that fellow, would you?" she asked me.

Women of my mother's generation never discussed sex. Neither I nor any of my friends received any heart-to-heart, "Dear, it's time I told you something," advice. Mother told me the nuns would tell me anything I needed to know. And in a way they did. When we were seniors, Mother St. Margaret locked the door of the classroom, looked out the window to make sure that Wilfred, the house eunuch, combination bus driver and general repair man, who lived over the carriage house, was nowhere within earshot. She then said that we were now sixteen and seventeen years of age and might be invited on dates.

Pray God, we thought.

"Sometimes the young man might be driving a car," she continued.

Pray God again.

"Sometimes the car may be crowded, and you might have to sit on a young man's lap."

We shivered with hope.

"Therefore, young ladies, if the occasion ever arises that you might have to get into a crowded car with a young man, be sure to bring a pillow."

She unlocked the door. My sole sex-education lesson was over.

Mother began making up the invitation list. Even after the experience with Uncle Fred at her own wedding, she hadn't learned. She kept digging up cousins I'd never met, inviting them because they were "family." Of course the budget was tight, but if we eliminated the soup, we'd save enough to have a lovely affair at the McAlpin Hotel. She had had her reception twenty-five years earlier at the Martinique, next door. And, of course, going hand in hand with all the time spent planning was my life as a Pan Am hostess.

Africa was still divided into territories: The Belgian Congo. The British Gold Coast. French West Africa. The Union of South Africa.

India had achieved its independence two years earlier, but the sense of colonialism remained in the very air we breathed.

I was on the last Pan Am flight into Prague before it was closed to western planes. Soviet Union soldiers with submachine guns guarded the terminal while we boarded seven American men who were anxious to get out of that country while they could.

On one flight, I brought over a four-year-old British child, Gillian Ann Richardson. Her father, an American service-

man, had gone home, leaving her mother pregnant. Gillian's mother was dying, and her best friend, a war bride, had been trying to adopt the girl. Finally the red tape had been cut through.

Gillian was a slender, quiet child with enormous brown eyes. She clung to the woman from the orphanage who had brought her to the plane. I asked the woman if she and Gillian had been very close. It was sad to learn that she had known the little girl for only twenty-four hours.

In flight training, we had been told that the passengers on the plane were our guests and should be treated as though they were in our private living rooms. We were not simply to serve meals. We were to chat with passengers and make them at ease. But on the long flight over the Atlantic, I still found time to sit with Gillian, to hold her when she fell asleep, to pray that her new life would be a happy one.

Gillian's arrival turned out to be a media event. At La-Guardia, the purser led the passengers across the tarmac. I was asked to wait with Gillian, then walk down the steps and hand her to her new mother. There was just one problem: Gillian by now had bonded to me. She clung to me and refused to let go.

"Look at her," I whispered. Her mother's best friend, her new mother, was an English beauty with strawberry blond hair, blue eyes, and a peaches-and-cream complexion. She had not seen Gillian in three years.

"I knew she'd grow to look exactly like this," she said, her face radiant with joy.

"Look at her, Gillian," I whispered.

They gazed at each other. Then Gillian reached out her arms and rushed down the steps of the plane.

On another occasion my special passenger from England was a woman whose calloused hands, worn expression, and shabby clothing were all the evidence needed of a hardworking life. She sat quietly, refusing the lunch tray with a shake of her head, but timidly requesting a cup of tea, if it wasn't too much trouble. I thought she might be terrified of flying and was trying not to be obvious about it. The seat next to her was empty, and when the other passengers were settled, I sat down beside her. She began to tell me about her daughter. She was a war bride. So in love. The most beautiful wedding. "I haven't seen her in three years," she said.

"And you're going to visit her now? How wonderful."

"I'll be bringing her back with me, but I'm not sure if she's ready yet."

"Will her husband be with her?"

"No, but I'll be seeing him now." She turned to me, her eyes filled with pain, her voice raw with grief. "He murdered her two days ago."

The television cameras were waiting on the tarmac for her, too.

I loved just about every minute of flying. Getting married meant I'd have to give up the job, because you had to be single to be a stewardess. But as my wedding day approached, I did not regret when the moment came to turn in my wings.

I was ready and eager for the next chapter in my life. Marriage. A family. And learning to become a professional writer.

December 26, 1949, was the big day. Our little prefab church had burned down a few years earlier and the new one hadn't been built yet, so the school auditorium was where Sunday Masses, weddings, and funerals were held. Some girls went to other churches for their weddings, but the pastor, Monsignor Quinn, considered that an act of total disloyalty. When Mother had received the telegram from the Navy Department that indicated Joseph had only a few days to live, she had rushed to the rectory. Monsignor had helped her to get a priority plane reservation and, from the proceeds of the Sunday collection, lent her the money for the ticket. She paid him back, but even so, I felt I owed it to him to get married in the auditorium. It was decorated with Christmas greens and poinsettias and did look Christmasy. They even had a big red bow on the basketball hoop directly in front of the stage where the Nuptial Mass was celebrated.

I spent my last few nights in the apartment on Lurting Avenue, figuring out the seating arrangements at the McAlpin. "Who in the name of God is this?" was the exasperated question I asked Mother a number of times as I studied the list of invitees. Her answer was always the same: "A cousin."

"I hope none of them is in sneakers," I grumbled. None of them was, but one little kid whose baby-sitter didn't show was brought along at the last minute, and his beaming parents persuaded him to sing a couple of songs for us.

"Happy is the bride that the sun shines on today," goes the old saying. Well the bride was happy, but the sun was in hiding. Sheets of pouring rain were being driven by near-gale winds. The service was being held only one block away from the apartment, and in the need to keep expenses chopped, we'd hired only one limo to make three runs. How long could it take? First Mother would be driven, then the bridesmaids, then Johnny and I. He was giving me away.

The problem was that each of us had to wait to make the dash across the sidewalk and into the limo between gusts of torrential rain, and that slowed up the timing. I was twenty-two minutes late. And there'd been another unpredictable hitch.

The organist was blind. He was in the choir loft and received his signal to switch to "Here Comes the Bride" by a buzzer an altar boy pushed from the side of the altar when the bride arrived.

Mrs. Clark was always ahead of time and was in the church at five of ten. The altar boy spotted her and pushed the buzzer. She walked down the aisle to the bridal march from *Lohengrin*. A second buzzer was pushed when the same dopey kid saw my mother arrive a few minutes later. Ditto the bridal march for her. When I arrived, I realized there was something odd. Then I got it. People were already standing up and facing the rear of the church.

Warr's first words to me at the foot of the altar were, "What kept you?"

Then, on the same stage where eleven years earlier I had not gotten the chance to say "Come let us dance to the music of this happy day," I took my wedding vows. And for the next fourteen years and nine months, until Warren's death, we lived happily ever after.

EIGHT

*A*partments in post-war New York were as scarce as hen's teeth. To ease the shortage, the Metropolitan Insurance Company had built two housing complexes in Manhattan between Fourteenth and Twenty-third Streets, from First Avenue east to Avenue C. The complex that ran from Fourteenth to Twentieth Street was called Stuyvesant Town. The complex from Twentieth to Twenty-third was called Peter Cooper Village and was more upscale, with apartments that had larger rooms and a second bath.

But both complexes were attractive, airy, and comfortable, and had plenty of playgrounds for the rapidly arriving post-war babies. Unlike many such housing projects, they also proved durable, and still—more than fifty years later—are sought-after housing, with long waiting lists.

The father of my new sister-in-law, June, was friendly with a Manhattan congressman. He had already helped June and

Allan to get an apartment in Stuyvesant Town, and now he promised to help us.

We got one. I was embarrassed, however, when we signed the lease. Another new tenant was there, almost hysterical with glee at getting a place. She and her husband had been living in a furnished room for three years while they waited for an apartment. "How long have you been waiting?" she asked.

"Forever," I assured her.

Johnny had graduated from high school and was working to save for college. Thanks to Joseph's G.I. insurance, and my mother's status as the dependent of a deceased serviceman, she had a monthly pension for life—small, but enough to take care of her basic expenses. She still baby-sat to make a little money, but in death, as in life, Joseph had taken care of her. She no longer aspired to having her old home back some-day—the apartment was more convenient and better suited to her needs, she decided. The bus which had replaced the trolley car arrived regularly right at the corner, and the church where she attended daily Mass was less than a block away.

Warren and I took to marriage as ducks to water. We loved each other, we were in love, we were best friends, and we made each other laugh. He was a very special man. Years later, one of his friends expressed it best: "Mary, he'd light up a room when he came into it." And it was true. He was good looking, smart, kind, funny, yet oddly enough, when he wasn't smiling, could look austere. I told him I was intrigued by the fact that he had

such a Waspy appearance, especially in winter when he wore a homberg and chesterfield.

Almost every man in Stuyvesant Town in those days was an ex-G.I. Many of them were going to law school or business school at night while working during the day. They were all starting to climb the ladder in their profession and all were sure they were going to make it. Warren had a job as salesman for American President Lines, the prestigious passenger and cargo steamship carrier that had offices in Rockefeller Center. He thoroughly enjoyed the travel business. The only catch was that he had begun to realize that a beautiful office, classy clients, and the ability to sail anywhere in the world free on vacations did not make up for a relatively low salary. He began to think about leaving his job there and trying another profession.

And I was aching, yearning, burning to write. I wanted to learn how to tell a story. I compare the experience of learning the craft of writing to that of a singer who has genuine talent but who needs to go to a conservatory to be taught to use her voice properly.

As soon as we returned from our honeymoon, I walked down to New York University and signed up for a course in short-story writing. William Byron Mowery, the teacher of the course I took, was an elfin-sized man who wore a tie so long that it gave the visual illusion of scraping the tops of his shoes. His talents as a teacher, however, were huge, and he set my feet firmly on the path that I had been seeking all my life.

"Write about what you know," he advised the class, then pointed to me. "You've been a Pan American stewardess. The magazines are getting stories from the pilot's point of view. Nobody's writing in the voice of the hostess. You should."

He continued the lecture. "I've heard it from all of you. You *know* you can write. You're *sure* you can write. But you don't know *what* to write. Now listen, because I'm going to solve that problem for you. Take a dramatic situation, something that sticks in your mind, something that happened to you or to someone you know, maybe something that you read in the paper that intrigued you. Ask yourself two questions, 'Suppose?' and 'What if?' and turn that situation into fiction."

His was advice that I'm still following, although I've added one more question: "Why?" In suspense/mystery, there's got to be a believable motive for the crime. If there are five people who might have committed a murder, only one of them would have been vengeful enough, jealous enough, psychotic enough to go over the line and take a life.

Bill Mowery taught us the basics of slick-magazine short-story writing: the compelling opening paragraph, the problem, the secondary but related problem, the three downward steps, the climax, the denouement. "Start thinking about writing your first short story," he warned. "That assignment is coming up soon."

So was something else. Six weeks after we were married, I,

who love coffee, complained that for some reason the coffee didn't taste good anymore.

"Oh, it can't be getting any worse," Warren said. "Promise me that."

"Very funny," I said. "It's the coffee, not the chef."

Marilyn, our firstborn, was on her way. I was to learn with all five pregnancies that the coffee tasting "off" was a signal that there was going to be another little stranger coming into our lives. The nurses at St. Vincent's Hospital, where I had my next four babies, became so aware of that fact that when I came down from the delivery room, they'd have a cup of coffee waiting. The minute the baby was born, coffee tasted wonderful again.

I became friendly with half a dozen other students in the class, and we decided to form a workshop, a move Professor Mowery heartily endorsed. We made up basic rules: meet once a week, there would be two readers an evening, who would read for up to twenty minutes each; a rotating chairperson would strictly enforce the time limit, allowing only an extra minute or two for the reader to complete a chapter or the last few pages of a short story.

Clockwise from the reader, each member of the group would comment for three minutes on what they had just heard. Not, "I love it, it's wonderful," but more on the order of, "I like your main character, but don't believe it is consistent for her to . . ."

After the first go-round, the listeners were entitled to add a quick additional thought, to agree or disagree with another member's comment; then it was the reader's turn to speak. He or she was not to justify but to respond to some of the points that had been raised, or, if appropriate, explain, "When I had the character make that statement, I was intending to fore-shadow . . ." and so forth. After about five minutes of general discussion on the manuscript, it was the second reader's turn.

We all lived in Manhattan, and each Wednesday evening, we met in a different home. Our five members became twelve almost overnight. Several members had already been pub-lished in magazines, and one senior member even had six nov-els to her credit.

Mowery gave us our first major assignment: each of us was to write a short story. Following his advice, I decided my main character would be a stewardess. But what was the most dramatic situation I had encountered while I worked at Pan Am? I asked myself.

Determining that took a nanosecond. It was that round-trip flight from London to Prague and back, just when the Soviet forces were closing Prague to Westerners. We carried no passengers on the first lap. When we arrived at the airport in Prague, we found that the Soviets were having a military air show, and there were thousands of spectators in the surround-ing area. When they spotted our plane, they turned as one from watching the aerial spectacle and waved and clapped and cheered. It was a stunning and heartfelt reception.

We landed and went inside the nearly deserted terminal to be greeted by Soviet guards carrying submachine guns. The passengers who were scheduled to fly with us to London— seven American men—were huddled together in a corner. I went over to them.

"No one would dare to see us off," one of them confided. "It is not wise to advertise your American connections."

The Captain came over. "Mary, don't wander off," he advised. "We're going to fuel up and get out. I don't like it here."

When we took off, all the spectators again turned away from the military formations. Below I saw a sea of faces looking up, but this time no one cheered or clapped. We had arrived to a tumultuous welcome. We departed in eerie silence.

One of our passengers was weeping. He pointed down. "There is no one in that crowd who wouldn't give half of the rest of his life to be in this plane," he told me.

Suppose? What if?

Suppose the flight hostess was the first to return to the plane. Suppose she found an eighteen-year-old member of the underground resistance, trying to hide on the plane? Suppose the Soviet military police are searching the field for him, and she knows they are heading toward her plane? Suppose the would-be stowaway pleads, "Help me. Help me."

I decided it was a good premise. I called my fictitious stowaway Joe and gave him my brother's shock of blond hair and blue eyes. It wasn't hard to emotionalize the need Carol, the fictitious hostess, felt to try to save him.

With Warren, on our honeymoon.

I turned in the story, and the next week Mowery called me aside. "You have written a professional story," he told me. "I absolutely guarantee you this is a story that will sell."

It did—six years and forty rejection slips later.

On the mornings of the fifteenth, and again on the last day of the month, all through Stuyvesant Town a clinking sound could be heard. Most of us were paid biweekly and usually by payday morning had literally run out of cash. On those days, the men on their way to work scraped together bus fare and lunch money by returning deposit bottles.

That was why on November 14, when Warren came home from work, and I told him I thought we'd better get to the hospital, our combined resources amounted to thirty-four cents. There were neither credit cards nor bank withdrawal facilities in 1950. The money we were saving for a house was in the bank, and the bank was closed. Mrs. Clark, who now lived in Manhattan, wasn't home. The labor pains were coming thick and fast. It was definitely time to get to the hospital, and the one at which my doctor practiced was in Westchester County, nearly an hour's drive away.

The quickest way was via the Triborough Bridge into the Bronx, but that cost a quarter in tolls. Somehow it didn't seem appropriate to arrive at the hospital for the birth of our first-born with only nine cents to our names. We crossed our fingers and took the Willis Avenue Bridge, which was free. We got as far as Yonkers, and the pains stopped. Just plain

stopped. I hadn't eaten a thing all day, and I suddenly realized I was starving.

The doctor had told me in no uncertain terms that once the pains started I was to check in at the hospital as soon as possible. "A first baby may take a lot of time, or it may come fast," he'd cautioned. I knew there wasn't a chance in the world that once I got to the hospital, they'd give me something to eat.

"Let's stop at a diner," I suggested.

Even in those days, thirty-four cents did not buy a meal fit for a king. We sat at the counter, studied the menu, and then ordered a bowl of cream of mushroom soup and two spoons because Warr was hungry, too. That meant twenty cents for the soup, plus a nickle tip, so even though we had taken the Willis Avenue Bridge, we still arrived at the hospital with only nine cents between the two of us.

Our firstborn took twenty-five hours of hard labor before she made her debut. In those days, the husband was told to kiss his wife good-bye and go home and have a good night's sleep. All through the next day, I could hear Warren's phone calls from the office and the nurse's chirpy reply: "Mrs. Clark is in active labor and progressing nicely."

In fact, Mrs. Clark was ready to take the gas pipe. By the time I was wheeled into the delivery room, I couldn't wait for the anesthesia. The concept of natural childbirth was nonexistent. At the moment of delivery, it was, "Bye-bye, Mother,"

and a cone was clamped over my face. Husbands never got near the delivery room. They were the well-rested creatures who stayed at home and received the call to come to the hospital and admire their offspring.

I've had five children and never consciously experienced a birth, a fact I've always regretted. But I clearly remember the first time each one of my children was put in my arms—five absolutely magical moments when I felt that I had touched the wondrous hand of God.

Unfortunately, that first time, I was sharing a room with Ruth somebody or other. Her brother-in-law, she proudly bragged, was the biggest bookie in Westchester County and was coming to visit. He arrived, a short, bull-shaped man in a striped suit, clenching a cigar between his teeth; he was accompanied by his bodyguard.

He took the cigar out for a moment. "The kid's cute, Ruth," he grunted.

"Yeah, cute," the bodyguard echoed.

I turned my head and closed my eyes, hoping they'd think I was asleep. After the difficult labor, I was running a fever, a shock reaction that would wear off in a few days, the doctor had assured me. Ruth let the brother-in-law know that the hospital was going to cost a fortune, got his promise to pick up the tab, then lowered her voice to a stage whisper that could have been heard in the next county: "Her name is Mary Clark. She's got milk fever because she's nursing the baby."

Milk fever? I'd heard about it before, but where? When

Ruth's elite visitors had departed, I asked her about it. "Milk fever happens when the milk backs up and hits your brain," she explained. "You go cuckoo. That's what's happening to you. When you leave the hospital, you won't go home. They'll take you directly to the nut house."

I remembered hearing Mother's story that when she was young, her friend had spent time in the asylum on Welfare Island, then a dreary spot in the East River adjacent to the Fifty-ninth Street Bridge. "Poor thing, it was right after the baby was born," was the way Mother and her cousins summed up the sad event. Later I learned that the lady had been suffering from acute postpartum depression and was hospitalized for only a short time, but listening to the medical expert in the other bed, I was sure that my mother's friend must have had milk fever and that now I had it, too, and my next stop was the asylum.

Unasked, Ruth confirmed that fear. "Welfare Island is where they take people like you. And don't ask your husband, because he won't tell you the truth," she cautioned. "He'll lie and tell you you're fine. Just the way the doctor is lying to you now. You're *not* fine. Anyone who has a fever after childbirth is going nuts."

The usual maternity stay was a week. I spent the entire time in total fear. Even though my fever began to recede, I was constantly assured by Ruth that the damage had already been done to my brain: "Your husband probably has made all the arrangements. I guess your mother will take care of the baby."

Wreathed with smiles, Warren arrived to pick up the baby and me. He was beaming, and he assured me he wasn't nervous, but I pointed out that his shoes didn't match—the right one was black, the left one brown. Could he look this happy if he was about to sign me into a mental hospital? I wondered.

This time we paid the quarter, drove over the Triborough Bridge, and started down the East Side Drive. I felt my heart pounding as we approached the turnoff to the Fifty-ninth Street Bridge and Welfare Island. Sixty-fifth, fourth, third, second, first, SIXTIETH Street! I waited. The turn signal did not go on. Five minutes later, we were pulling into a parking space outside our Stuyvesant Town apartment building.

"I'm so glad to be here!" I said, with a big sigh of relief.

Warren stared at me. "Did you think you were going to the movies?"

I told him the "milk fever" story.

Four months later the coffee started to taste rotten again. Warren and I agreed that this time, after the baby was born, I'd be in a private room.

Warren and me with our family on Easter Sunday 1959. From the left:
Marilyn, Patty, Warren Jr., Carol, and David.

NINE

*P*itter, patter, pitter, patter. Warren Francis Clark, Jr., arrived thirteen months after Marilyn. I brought him home on Christmas Eve, which was also my twenty-fourth birthday. Two days later, Warren and I celebrated our second wedding anniversary. Our thirteen-month-old was teething, our infant colicky. We each held a wailing offspring as we clinked champagne glasses.

David checked in two years later. The city marked his debut by beginning alternate side of the street parking regulations, something we had failed to pay attention to. When it was time to go to the hospital we found that the car had been towed away. Fortunately we no longer had to drive out to Westchester; St. Vincent's Hospital was only a five-minute cab ride from home.

We had quickly outgrown the one-bedroom apartment. Now we outgrew the two-bedroom unit as well. During the

day, the living room looked like a day-care center. Our three offspring were bunkered in the second bedroom, which was never intended to accommodate two cribs and a youth bed.

One day I couldn't get the whole bunch of us into the elevator. Marilyn was pushing her doll stroller, Warrie was riding his fire engine, Dave was in the carriage, I was dragging a shopping cart, and I was pregnant again.

Warr and I both loved living in Manhattan, but we had to have more room. That night I said, "Dear heart, do not plan to play golf on Saturday. We are going house hunting."

By then I had eleven short stories in the mail. The one Professor Mowery had said would surely sell was making its way through every publishing house listed in *Writer's Market*. In those days, I was so dumb I thought that being a subscriber to the magazine might just tip the balance in my favor. Therefore my usual letter began something like this:

Dear Editor Smith-Jones,

I am enclosing a short story entitled "Stowaway," circa 3,500 words, which I thought might be appropriate for your fine magazine to which I have a subscription. It concerns the attempts of a flight hostess to stow a young member of the underground aboard her flight and bring him safely to freedom. . . .

I look forward to hearing from you.

I did hear from Smith-Jones and all the other editors, usually by return mail. The arrival of my self-addressed and stamped eight-and-a-half-by-eleven envelopes, each containing a scorned literary effort and the editor's printed rejection slip, was a regular event in my life. I could picture all of the editors, laughing maniacally as they dropped my offerings into their out boxes. Wait and see, I vowed. Wait and see.

Meanwhile, on the floor beneath our tiny slot of a mailbox in the lobby of the apartment building, a pile of weekly and monthly magazines was steadily growing. After all, in good conscience I couldn't claim to have a subscription to a magazine if I didn't actually have a subscription, could I? Tell the truth and shame the devil.

For the first eight or ten stories, I continued to use the flight-hostess background. Oddly enough, the first two, "Stowaway" and "Milk Run," were suspense stories. "Milk Run" came about because for two weeks during my Pan Am days I flew the so-called "honeymoon express" to Bermuda. That involved taking off from LaGuardia at eight in the morning, arriving in Bermuda at noon, hanging around the airport there, then returning in the late afternoon.

We all considered that assignment a pain in the neck. In the morning, we had to serve breakfast to rapturous newlyweds who were linking arms, holding hands, or smooching so much that it was impossible to find a spot between or around them to place a tray. In the afternoon, we brought back the returning lovey-dovies, who toasted each other with cham-

pagne by entwining their arms and sipping from each other's glasses.

Bob Considine, a famous journalist, was on assignment in Bermuda and had an agreement with Pan Am that the flight hostess would carry his nationally syndicated column on the return flight to New York and give it to a courier who would be waiting at the airport. One day it was my turn to make the delivery. When my plane landed, Warren picked me up at La-Guardia, and we drove to a diner in the Bronx for a snack. Over our second cup of coffee, I chatted about the day and then realized to my horror that I had totally forgotten about meeting the courier and still had the column in my flight bag.

Fortunately the address of the *Daily Mirror,* 405 West Forty-second Street, was on the envelope. We raced down to Manhattan and stopped in front of the tired-looking building that housed the newspaper. A sleepy guard opened his eyes long enough to tell me where to go, and I took a rickety elevator to the editorial floor.

It was empty except for a man hunched over a desk and wearing a green eyeshade. He looked up at me. "What do you want, girlie?"

Clearly he was in a filthy mood. I pulled the envelope from my uniform bag and held it out. "I've got Bob Considine's column," I began timidly.

"*Considine's column!*" he bellowed. He grabbed the phone, dialed, and barked, "Hold it. We've got Considine." Then he looked at me. "You going back to Bermuda tomorrow?"

"Yes."

"Tell Considine to get his column in on time."

Suppose the stewardess has a journalist boyfriend who gives her a list of all the servicemen missing in Korea and the camps where they are being held? What if it's stolen from her during the flight?

That "Suppose? . . . What-if? . . . Why?" story became "Milk Run." Ironically, when eventually it was published, it was back to back in the magazine with an article by Bob Considine. If you only knew, I thought, as I mentally gave him a grateful tip of the hat.

Except for those two stories, I was writing the boy-meets-girl variety that were so popular in the women's magazines of the day, of course using my flight background. "Million-Mile Stewardess," "The Marriage Junket," "Captain, Dear, Come Home with Me," "Love Can Be a Hubbly-Bubbly," "Reach High for Happiness"—these were some of the titles.

Eventually, I started to get not just form rejection slips, but slips with scrawled comments on the bottom, on the order of, "Not right for us, but try us again." At least they know I'm alive, I thought exultantly. In those Madison Avenue offices where those rarefied godly creatures live, they're becoming aware of me. They hear me knocking at the door.

No one could have been more supportive of my efforts than Warren. He willingly minded the kids the nights I went to the writers' workshop, but in his mind, writing was a hobby, and his concern was that eventually I'd be crushed by all the

rejections. "Look at it this way," he would urge when yet another self-addressed envelope arrived. "It's a hobby that gives you great pleasure. Some women play bridge. You write."

Warr's concern was genuine. He didn't want me to be hurt, and I understood that. When budding writers start submitting manuscripts and begin getting rejections in return, their families often fall into one of two traps. They either say, "Honey, don't break your heart. Give it up," or "You're the best writer in the world, and the reason these people aren't publishing you is because they're so busy publishing their friends." Neither response, however well intentioned, is helpful. That's the reason it's great for budding writers to be in workshops. Their fellow members understand that a personal comment from an editor really may be significant.

Someone in our workshop sold a story to Collier's magazine, then one of the leading weeklies, for the princely sum of one thousand dollars. We were all thrilled and began the custom of having a cake with a candle to celebrate when a member sold something. I, however, continued to get nothing but rejection slips and the occasional "Try us again" notes of encouragement.

Then one day I picked up the mail, opened my self-addressed envelope, and read the scrawled line at the bottom of the rejection slip: "Mrs. Clark, your stories are light, slight, and trite."

Oh, pardon me while I pull out the knife, I thought. I was on my way to Hanscom's bakery around the corner. To rev up

business, Hanscom's was running a contest in all its New York outlets. The wall behind the counter held large pictures of four cocktail dresses, a Givenchy, a Chanel, a Dior, and one by God knows what other designer. The dresses were the wasp waist, crinoline-lined, ankle-length creations so popular in the mid-1950s.

The entry blanks were on the counter. The instructions for the contest were to complete the following sentence in twenty-five words or less: I choose the (fill in name of designer) because _____.

While my three- and four-year-olds tried to fish Popsicles out of the ice-cream freezer, and the baby pulled my hair, the clerk held down the entry blank. I wrote:

> *I choose the Givenchy because I have three young children and it's been a long time since I've felt irresistible. I'm sure in that gown, I could feel irresistible plus!*

A week later the phone rang. I had won the contest! It was the first visible proof that I was a writer. I loved that dress and wore it to all the grand occasions, being careful whenever possible to drop in the information that I'd won it in a writing contest. When it went out of style, I packed it away carefully, tissue-wrapped, in a box. There it stayed until years later when Carol, age ten, came down from the attic one day wearing it. It was Halloween. She coupled it with a pointed hat and went trick-or-treating garbed as a witch. Her costume won a prize.

*   *   *

When we started househunting, we made the usual rounds: Westchester, Connecticut, Long Island, New Jersey. Warren's brother Allan and his wife, June, had moved to the Township of Washington in northern New Jersey. When we visited them, we decided we liked the area very much. New Jersey is a historic state, steeped in the history of the Revolution, and it is also beautiful. It has mountains and lakes and one of the longest shorelines along the Atlantic of any state on the East Coast. At the time, it also had an unattractive stretch on the New Jersey Turnpike by which, unfortunately, most visitors judged it. That area has been pretty well cleaned up now, but comedians still like to give the Garden State a kick when they can't come up with fresh material.

It has always amused me that I've had to defend the two places where I've spent most of my life, the Bronx and New Jersey. When I hear either one of them belittled, I think of an expression Warren's mother used. "When you know better, you'll do better." I also point out that there are only three major locations in the world that are preceded by "The": The Vatican, The Hague, and The Bronx.

Our first house was a typical starter home, designed in the Cape Cod style; it consisted of a living room, two bedrooms, kitchen with dining area, and one bath. It also had an unfinished attic for future expansion. We decided to take the plunge and spend the extra sixteen hundred dollars to have the builder finish the two upstairs bedrooms and bath imme-

diately, but to be economical we decided to paint and wall-paper them ourselves.

There was only one problem. Neither Warren nor I had the least aptitude for this kind of endeavor. He started paint-ing the upstairs bedrooms, knocked over the can, and walked downstairs to get a rag to mop up the mess, leaving bright yellow footprints on the new carpet. Then he poured the left-over paint down the sink. The Roto-Rooter man eventually managed to reopen the drains. With equal ineptitude, I wall-papered the upstairs bathroom but hung the paper upside down. The pattern was fish swimming through a tropical sea. Upside-down, the fish took on a malevolent, eerie look that actually was an icebreaker when we had parties. "Do you real-ize . . . ? " Or "Did you do that on purpose? How interesting."

A dozen years later, when Warren Jr. and David were in high school, they came home one day looking tremendously pleased with themselves. "Dad would be so proud of us, Mom," they reported. "In mechanical ability, we both came out untrainable."

It's genetic on both sides. My father's sole household chore had been to shake down the ashes and shovel coal onto the fire before he left for work. Upstairs, we would hold our breath waiting for his plaintive wail from the basement, "Dammit, Nora, I have put the fire out." It happened regularly, but he al-ways sounded surprised.

Then, four months after we moved into the new house, the morning came when the mail included a letter from *Ex-*

tension magazine. I had "Stowaway" in submission there. Was it possible? I wondered. It was my peaceful post-breakfast, cup-of-tea half-hour. Warren was off at work, Marilyn was in kindergarten, the boys were in the next room playing and not yet fighting. I was seven months pregnant, hence tea rather than coffee.

I propped the unopened envelope against the sugar bowl. Was it possible? Could it really be possible? Had I finally sold a story?

No, I told myself. My subscription to *Extension* has run out. They want me to renew.

But, on the other hand, they don't type the renewal notices individually or use such good-quality paper.

Maybe it's a nicer way for them to say, "Try us again."

On the other hand, they didn't return the manuscript.

It was time to learn my fate. I slit the envelope open and read the encosed letter. *Extension* magazine offered to purchase my story "Stowaway" for one hundred dollars!

I've received some pretty dazzling contract offers over the years, but never, ever, ever, have I been so thrilled as I was to learn that I had sold that first short story. The letter of acceptance is framed in my study.

The name of the protagonist in "Stowaway" was Carol. Two months later we gave that name to our newborn baby girl. Today, she points out that it's a good thing the main character's name wasn't Hepzibah, because if it had been, that's un-

doubtedly the name she'd have been stuck with. She also believes that she must have felt the excitement of that sale in the womb because she's the only one of my children who grew up to be a bestselling suspense writer herself.

After that initial breakthrough, the short-story sales began to happen with increasing regularity. *Extension* also bought "Milk Run," the story inspired by my goofing up the delivery of Bob Considine's column. *McCall's* bought "The Marriage Junket." Smaller regional magazines started picking me up regularly. When I reported that first sale to *Extension* to the workshop, one of our new members, a woman who had published eight novels, told her agent, Patricia Schartle Myrer, about me. Pat invited me to come in to her office. When I arrived, she announced she had decided to represent me. She was a young agent. I was a young writer. Being taken on by her proved to be the kindness of the gods. Pat had been a senior editor before becoming an agent, and when I turned in a story to her, she made me rewrite and rewrite until she felt I had it in shape. That process continued for nearly twenty years, until Pat retired. Our last child is named Patricia Mary after a winning combination.

My mother never quite forgave us for moving to New Jersey. Warren urged her to live with us and avoid the endless bus trips back and forth, but even though we gave her carte blanche to come with all her beloved furniture, there was never the faintest chance she'd move. You only had to drive

her halfway across the George Washington Bridge to have her start sniffing the air and remarking on the heavenly breezes that originated in the Bronx.

She delighted in being a grandmother. She had a deep horror of my leaving the children with a young baby-sitter and thought nothing of taking the two-hour, three-bus trip to New Jersey to mind them.

From the time any of the children could toddle half a block without falling, my mother was whisking them on the Circle Line Tour, or taking them to the Central Park Zoo, to the Statue of Liberty, and to parades and to beaches. She especially adored amusement parks. In 1939, the summer my father died, she took Joe and John and me to the World's Fair. I can still see her long mourning veil trailing wraithlike behind her as we plunged down on the parachute jump. A quarter of a century later, when she was seventy-six, she was taking my five offspring on the steeplechase at Coney Island.

Long years of making one dollar do the work of ten couldn't be unlearned, and if the kids had any complaint, it was that Nanny made them share a soda or divide a sandwich in the Automat. She once promised my then five-year-old that she'd take him up to the top of the Empire State Building. Upon realizing that she had to pay for the tickets to the Observation Tower, she whisked him up on the business elevator to the eighty-sixth floor, stood him at a window, and said brightly, "Here we are at the top. Isn't this fun?"

Mother was adamant that the children not miss out on any

important excursions. One day, her voice distressed, she came out with, "Warren, do you realize your children have never been to Bear Mountain?"

To which he replied with a smile, "Mrs. Higgins, I think they'll survive."

Her caring for the children encompassed Warren and me. She adored Warr, and to her, "himself" was the grandest husband any girl could have. "The disposition of a saint," she'd say with a sigh. "I hope you know how lucky you are, Mary." The only times she wavered in her devotion to him was during my pregnancies, when, totally unconsciously, and to our great amusement, Mother would refer to Warren as "that fellow."

Those first years in that first house were filled with promise. Warren was working for Northwest Orient Airlines. I was selling short stories. If there was one cloud in our sky, it was that I began to be uneasy about Warren's health. It seemed to me that for a man just turning forty, especially one who'd been a splendid athlete, he could tire too easily and looked drained and pale at the end of the day.

Something he had said when we were engaged kept replaying in my mind. He had told me that when he was about twelve years old, a certainty had come over him that he was not going to live a long life. At the time I'd said something like, "Every kid gets that feeling at that age," but even then I'd had a foreboding that for him it was different.

Labor Day 1959 dawned picture perfect. In just about every backyard, families were barbecuing and visiting back

and forth. Our neighbor across the street had decided to pull down a dead tree. He was having a hard time, and the men from the surrounding houses, Warren included, went over to give him a hand. "One, two, three, heave." It turned out to be a difficult job. The wives watched with an indulgent "boys will be boys" smile as the guys pulled and strained to weaken the roots of the tree.

The next day Warr began to have chest pains. He kept insisting it was just a pulled muscle, but a couple of weeks later, he finally went to the doctor. Tests followed. He was told that the arteries leading to his heart were almost totally clogged; that the pains he was experiencing were caused by severe and advanced angina; that it was a miracle he hadn't had a fatal seizure when he strained to pull down the tree; that down the road there might be surgery for his condition, but for now he must consider himself a likely candidate for a heart attack. Always have nitroglycerin tablets in your pocket, he was instructed. Never run for a bus. Don't carry a heavy suitcase. Don't roughhouse with the children.

I, too, went to see his doctor that day, and I heard the same diagnosis. On the way home, I stopped at church, where I prayed, "Please let him live." The answer I heard was, "Come, take up your cross and follow Me."

That night, when Warren came home from work, the kids jumped all over him, the baby crawled to him, and I held out the cocktail I had waiting. We toasted each other. Whatever time we had left, we'd make it great.

He had three heart attacks in the next five years, but his sense of humor never dimished. "I don't worry about you," he'd say when we'd talk about the future. "You could be in rags in Detroit at midnight, and by sunup be well-dressed, with a hundred bucks in your pocket, and have done it honestly. Do me just one favor. Don't be a blooming widow. I mean, try to look gaunt for a while after I die."

No one loved life more than he did, and no one left it more gracefully. When that final attack took Warren from us, a part of my being went dark and did not brighten again for thirty-two years, not until I met and married John Conheeney, my second spouse extraordinaire.

At home with Warren and the kids, 1961.

TEN

Our world had begun to turn upside down even before Warren died. He had the first major heart attack in 1962. The night he was discharged from the hospital, we received a phone call. John's third child, my godchild, fifteen-month-old Laura Mary Higgins, had been killed in a fall from the fifth floor window of their apartment building. Soon after that, John and his wife, Maureen, separated. There was too much grief to hold under one roof.

In August 1964, Warren had his second heart attack. When he was finally released from the hospital on September nineteenth, it was obvious that his condition was deteriorating rapidly. He was suffering constant angina pains and taking countless nitroglycerin pills.

I had a good friend, Liz Pierce, who wrote syndicated radio programs, four-minute vignettes that were broadcast from Monday through Friday over three to five hundred

stations. Her series was essentially a publicity promotion vehicle for *Life* magazine. She would get advance copy of future articles, features, the kind that aren't immediate news and condense them for broadcast. Several times when Liz was on vacation, I had been asked to fill in for her, and as a result I had been offered a series of my own by her company. I declined. Writing five scripts a week was a heavy schedule, and I knew it would leave me with no time for the short stories.

But on September twenty-sixth, I called Liz and told her that if a new radio series came up, I *would* take it on if they'd have me. I told her that I was sure Warren did not have more than a year to live and that he was far too sick ever to work again.

Liz and Warr were great buddies. Only that morning a package she had sent him arrived in the mail. The note said, "Dear Warr, I hear you're going to be laid up for a while so tried to find *A History of Orgies* to entertain you. However, couldn't find one so hope this will make an acceptable substitute." She had sent Florence Aadland's book about her daughter, Beverly, the fifteen-year-old who was Errol Flynn's companion when he died.

The book has one of the best opening lines I've ever read: "I don't care what anyone says, my baby was a virgin when she met Errol Flynn." Warren loved it.

Liz told me that one of the writers at her company, a journalist, was moving to the west coast, and his series, *Portrait of a Patriot*, vignettes about well-known people who had in

some way made significant contributions through government, medicine, science, or the arts, was available. I told her that if they'd have me, I'd take it on.

It turned out Warren didn't have a year or even six months. He died that evening. His mother was visiting. It's funny, I always called her "Mom," but when I speak or write about her now, I refer to her as "Mrs. Clark." She was a dream mother-in-law, kind and generous. As a young girl, I had admired her from afar when I'd see her at the 12:15 Mass. There was something about her majestic carriage and stately appearance that commanded instant respect. When Warren and I got together, I quickly came to love her dearly.

She had been widowed two years before our marriage, and her sons were the center of her existence. Ken and his wife, Irene, had moved to Washington Township as well, and we lived within walking distance of each other. The fact that her twelve grandchildren were more like brothers and sisters than cousins delighted her.

She did not deceive herself about Warren's condition. Several times during that week in September after he came home, she told a friend that she would not want to outlive one of her sons. She was visiting the night he suffered the fatal attack; she collapsed at his bedside. When the doctor arrived, they were both gone.

For the children, it was a crushing double blow. In the same moment they had lost the father they adored and Mimi, as they called their beloved grandmother. At only ages five,

eight, ten, twelve, and thirteen, they had been introduced to profound grief.

I took all of them, even Patty and Carol, to the funeral parlor. The older ones understood death, but I was afraid that the little ones might not. When Warren was in the hospital, Patty would stand at the window waiting for him to come home. I felt she needed the finality of knowing that he wasn't coming home anymore.

The wake was enormously sad, but even in such dire circumstances, there can be a moment of levity.

Warren hated the expression, "I'm sorry for your trouble," a condolence frequently offered at Irish family wakes.

"You're sorry someone is *experiencing* trouble," he would point out.

A visitor came into the funeral parlor, looked at the two caskets, pressed my hand, and said, "I'm sorry for your *double* trouble."

I was afraid to turn around. I was sure Warren would have a pained expression on his face.

The evening of the funeral, I knew I needed to be by myself. My mother was exhausted and went home to rest. People had surrounded us for the last three days, but they understood my need for quiet time now. When the children went to bed, I sat in the tall fireside chair that had at one time graced the parlor in my mother's childhood home. I was beyond tears. For the moment, they had all been shed.

This is the rest of my life, I thought. I knew how much the

children would miss Warr. My heart ached for them. I knew about all the birthdays and holidays and graduations when they would see other kids with their fathers. I knew because I'd been there.

Warren had been so proud of them. They'd all done some professional acting and modeling. That had started when we lived in Stuyvesant Town and the first two were little. Someone I knew casually told me that her toddler was paid ten dollars an hour to model for the Sears Roebuck catalog. Ten dollars an hour! I couldn't believe it. She suggested that my offspring were just the type the Conover Agency wanted.

I phoned the agency, was invited in for an interview with the kids, and a week later one of them was booked for a job. The modeling calls came off and on for years. Warrie was the baby in monthly ads for the Bayer Aspirin series; Patty was a Gerber baby; Carol did a commercial for Quaker Oats; Marilyn for Ideal Toys; Dave had been the voice of Linus on the Ford Falcon radio commercials from the time he was four years old until he was seven, and Warren got such a kick out of seeing them on television. I'd been glad to have a little extra money to squirrel away against the day it might be needed. There were expenses, of course: clothing; trips to New York for "go-sees" that might or might not end up in a booking; composite pictures for the agency to disperse. Everything added up, but I'd still managed to save some money.

Warrie had just started the first grade when he became in demand for television commercials. By then we were

living in New Jersey, and I'd explained to the principal at St. Andrew's that I'd appreciate it if sometimes he could be excused from class early for a "go-see" and occasionally be absent for a day or two to act in a commercial. She agreed, with the proviso that it was not too frequent and that he keep his marks up.

A new parish was created in Washington Township with the result that the younger children, beginning with David, went to a different school, Our Lady of Good Counsel. When I timidly told the principal that I'd like to be able occasionally to have him excused either early or for a whole day, she looked at me severely. "Does he get paid for this activity?"

"Yes, he gets paid quite well," I replied.

"Can they use a nun?" she asked.

I'd always sworn that there would be no fudging of the truth. I'd never call in sick for them when they were working, and I never did. But one day when I was racing eight-year-old Warren in for a "go-see," as we exited the George Washington Bridge, he turned to me and asked, "What am I today, Mom, a big six or a small ten?"

Dave, an easygoing, happy-go-lucky child, had a plaintive quality about him. As skinny as one side of eleven when he was little, he always managed to look forlorn. His blond hair fell over his forehead, he wore a look of perpetual worry, and there was a beseeching note in his voice. You always felt you wanted to help him, although in no defined way.

One day when he was four, I had a "go-see" with him for

what I was told would be a public service ad. I was asked to bring in a selection of worn and shabby clothes. I scouted around and arrived with two suitcases laden with castoffs, which I offered to show the photographer.

He looked at Dave. The hair I had carefully combed was falling over Dave's eyes. He was wearing a new shirt and shorts. The shirt drooped over his shoulders, the waistband of the shorts was anchored on his skinny hips. One sock had somehow managed to get sucked under the heel of his shoe.

The photographer nodded approvingly. "He's perfect the way he is," he told me. He got Dave in position next to a little girl about his age and directed him to put his arm around her shoulder and to try to look sad. Dave let his mouth droop forlornly, but the photographer wasn't getting what he wanted. Then he had an inspiration: "Dave, will you please stretch out your hand and show me your happiest smile?"

David willingly agreed. The shoot was for United Way, and Dave's picture, wistful and pleading, appeared in ads all over the country. The caption under his image was "Give until it hurts."

I smiled, thinking of Warren's reaction to driving over the George Washington Bridge every evening for weeks and seeing that image of his son on a big billboard.

I thought of the fun we had had over my Fab commercial. The Ted Bates Advertising Agency had a new campaign for the soap powder Fab and wanted to use real mothers rather than models in the commercials. I got to their offices and was

given a form to fill out. It said something to the effect that I was to give my reasons why I used only Fab, never anything but Fab, in my washing machine.

Oh, please, I thought, but decided to go along. Tongue in cheek, I wrote that Fab made my clothes whitey-white and cleany-clean. Since there were a dozen other potential real life models there, I was sure I was wasting my time.

Finally it was my turn for the audition. It was already late, and I knew I'd be caught in five o'clock traffic. The interviewer asked if it was all right if he recorded me and assured me that I was being paid ten dollars whether or not I was chosen.

On tape I earnestly repeated what I had written. That wasn't quite enough. "Maybe there's one special reason why you use Fab?" he suggested.

I came up with one. "My son is a little league pitcher, and when he comes home after a game, his uniform is ever so dirty. Oh my goodness. I don't know how I'd get it clean without good old Fab."

"A little league pitcher," the interviewer said thoughtfully. "Fab and the little league pitcher. I like that." He smiled. "Then, Mrs. Clark, you are saying that you are happiest when you use Fab in your washing machine."

"I *never* want to see anything in my washing machine except All," I said emphatically, then immediately realized my mistake. *All* soap powder was the big competition! "*FAB!*" I screamed.

For the next week I had fun telling everyone how I had

blown my big chance to be a television star. Then I got a call from the modeling agency, instructing me to go to the Paramus, New Jersey, shopping mall on the following Friday for a test commercial. I would be paid the princely sum of twenty-five dollars for the day's work.

I got to the mall at eight in the morning. And I waited. And waited. And waited. At four o'clock, it was finally my turn. By then I was coffee-logged, bored, and disgusted. They gave me a shopping cart loaded down with boxes of Fab and told me to push it past the cameras. Then their spokesperson, the TV announcer Jack Lescoulie, came onto the scene. He admired the Fab hanging out of the basket and asked me why I had purchased it.

With exaggerated emphasis, I did my little league uniform story. The director ordered me to do it again, curtly telling me that I neither sounded nor looked spontaneous. During the day the weather had changed dramatically. By then it was windy and cold. The director was wearing earmuffs, heavy leather gloves, and a fur-lined jacket. I had on a spring coat, and my teeth were chattering. "Loosen up, Mrs. Clark," he snapped. "Do something natural. For example, if you want to scratch your nose, go right ahead."

"Have you given any consideration to my picking it?" I snapped back. We did one more take, and he abruptly dismissed me. I was sure the film of my audition would end up in the nearest trash can.

A few weeks later, a friend called. She'd just seen me in a

commercial on the *I Love Lucy* show! That commercial also ran on the top daytime soap operas for weeks. Warren and I went to Hawaii on the loot I made, and we had a marvelous time.

So many marvelous times . . .

As I sat there, I realized how important it was that I do a good job on the script writing. Because of Warren's heart condition, we had been able to get very little insurance. I knew that I certainly wasn't going to be able to support five children on short-story writing.

For a couple of years, I'd had significant success selling my short stories. *The Saturday Evening Post* was the pinnacle for mainstream writers in those days, and I not only had sold a short story there, but it had been included in their list of "Best *Post* Stories of the Year." Called "Beauty Contest at Buckingham Palace," it depicted a fictitious beauty contest among the very attractive young women who in 1961 were either a first lady, a reigning monarch, or the wife of a reigning monarch. They included Jackie Kennedy, Queen Elizabeth II, Queen Sirikit of Thailand, Queen Fabiola of Belgium, Queen Farah of Iran, and Princess Grace of Monaco. Not only to sell to the *Post,* but to be included as the author of one of its ten best stories of the year was a breathtaking achievement for me.

On the other hand, my first attempt at longer fiction had become a private joke. I'd aimed it at *Redbook,* which each month paid a princely sum of seven thousand dollars for a novella. Katie Miles, the stewardess who was the reason Joan

Murchison and I applied for jobs in Pan Am, had at that point gone through five husbands. The third was a Pan Am captain whom she thoughtfully removed from his wife when they were stationed in London.

I wrote that story from the wife's viewpoint—"the patient Griselda," as Professor Mowery referred to that kind of heroine, the long-suffering wife. In the story I wrote, she willingly gives the cheating husband a divorce; she loves him too much to stand in his way, and she won't take any alimony. I called that story "Journey Back to Love." The response from *Redbook*'s editors was, "We found the heroine as boring as her husband had."

The story did sell eventually to an English magazine and was published as a two-part serial, for which I was paid four hundred and fifty dollars, not seven thousand. But when the first installment came, I was thrilled to see I had the magazine's center spread, which is top-drawer positioning for a writer.

"Journey Back to Love" was blazoned across the double-spread. My name had never been larger in print. The illustration was of a sweet, sad creature weeping as she gazes out a rain-drenched window. The caption read, "Can a woman lose her husband's love when she offers him tenderness and obedience?" When Warren saw that, his comment to me was, "I certainly wish *you'd* try."

The memory made me laugh. True, I hadn't offered him obedience, but I certainly had given tenderness.

But the practical problems that were looming for me and my family inevitably came to mind. The fiction market had dried up, simply vanished. *Collier's* was out of business. *The Saturday Evening Post* now published only nonfiction. The women's magazines had dropped fiction and began printing nothing but self-help articles. "How to be your own best friend" . . . "How to grow a better lawn" . . . "How to be a helpful neighbor." How to do anything except sell fiction.

In the first nine months of 1964, I'd made a total of fifty dollars, the amount paid for the reprint of a short story. Warr had been joking that he'd been supporting an indigent writer. I knew that Liz was writing three radio series. That meant she was earning three hundred dollars a week. I resolved to get to that point, too.

At home, I was going to have to assume the role of both parents. And as my mother hadn't taken my father's death out on us, I resolved I wouldn't take my grief out on my children. As best I could, I would try to give them a happy home.

Finally, exhausted, I got out of the tall chair and went upstairs to bed. The room that was now only mine felt empty and quiet. I lay there for a long time, then finally dozed off. Around one in the morning, my bedroom door opened. Five-year-old Patty came in, dragging her security blanket. "Can I sleep with you?" she asked.

I scooped her up. "It's the best offer I've had all night," I told her. And we fell asleep together.

ELEVEN

*F*ollowing Warren's instructions to look gaunt after his death, I elected to wear black, at least until spring. It was not that I was locked into the old custom of wearing mourning attire, but he absolutely hated to see me dressed in black. By wearing it now, I felt I was fulfilling his admonition not to be a "blooming widow."

And so it was that five days after the funeral, clad in a black suit, I went into what I will now refer to as the Gordon R. Tavistock office on East Fifty-fifth Street to sign an agreement to write sixty-five four-minute programs for the *Portrait of a Patriot* series to be aired in thirteen-week cycles.

The office occupied the back half of the third floor of a brownstone located midway between Madison and Park Avenues. My friend Liz worked there, and she filled me in on the fact that the front half of the floor was a residential apartment occupied by another lady of easy virtue who each day

walked her toy poodle on Park Avenue and returned with a number of appointments from gentlemen who had stopped to chat with her.

There were only about seven people who actually worked in the brownstone office, including Liz, who was the head writer; Frank, head of sales; Barry, producer/director of the programs; Laurence, the office manager; an accountant whose name I forget; and a couple of typists. The other writers, free-lance like me, were hired by the series and worked at home.

Liz had explained that Gordon R. Tavistock—"G.R." as she called him—had made a bundle of money on a very popular television talent show and had conceived the idea of creating free-of-charge radio programming that would be distributed to radio stations but would have an essential difference from other so-called "filler" material. The stations would agree to schedule the Tavistock series at a specific time each day, and because the programs were hosted by a well-known personality, the publicity messages built into the announcements were deemed acceptable.

I was told I would meet Bud Collier, the host of my series, at the first recording session. Liz assured me that I shouldn't be nervous—Bud was a gem.

It was a while before I got to meet G.R. He hated living in New York, which he had decided was full of hippies. He was traveling around the country, looking for a suitable place to live. I immediately got the impression that G.R. was not as easygoing, as unflappable a boss as Sterling Hiles had been.

Laurence, the office manager, a thin, tall, pale, solemn man, who looked twenty years older than his actual age of forty-seven or eight, gave me sample scripts the former writer had done and asked me to submit a list of ten potential patriots for approval by the Grolier Company, the sponsor of the series. He said that I would be expected to be in the studio when the programs were recorded, in case alterations to the script were necessary. Finally, in a dirgelike voice, he welcomed me to the G. R. Tavistock family.

On the way out, I heard the lady of easy virtue in the front apartment arguing with the laundry delivery service. "I gave you sixteen sheets last week," she was shrieking, "and you only brought back fifteen."

I could tell I would now be traveling in a very sophisticated world.

It is not always how we act, but how we *react* that tells the story of our lives. . . . Laugh and the world laughs with you . . . God is in His Heaven, and if sometimes he seems not to be listening, it's only because He's saving something special for us. . . .

No matter how you slice it, the first year after losing your husband can only be compared to walking barefoot through hell. And it's just as bad for the children. The loss they have experienced is visible in their eyes.

Daily Mass helped get me through it. "I will go unto the altar of God, the God who gave joy to my youth." Family and

friends did their best to help. My brother-in-law Allan stopped in every evening on the way home from work. He was a rock for all of us. Mother was there 90 percent of the time, and while she was an enormous help, her presence also created an exasperating, but funny, problem.

Now that I was widowed, in her mind she wasn't only minding my five children. She immediately resumed her role as guardian of another young girl—me.

A week after Warren's death, Paul Becker, the funeral director, came in to drop off some Social Security application forms for me to fill out. When he arrived, Mother herded the boys upstairs. Patty and Carol were already in bed. In five minutes my visitor was gone, and Marilyn, who had just started her freshman year in high school, turned on her French-language records. For the next thirty minutes, a suave masculine voice asked such questions as *"Voulez vous aller à la bibliothèque avec moi?"*

When Marilyn finally turned off the record, Mother rushed down the stairs, indignation etched in every line of her face. "Mary, what was that fellow doing talking French to you?" she demanded.

I pointed out that Becker was married to a mortician and asked how I could possibly compete, given their shared interests. "Why just imagine how the two of them must bat the breeze at the end of the day," I told her.

But Paul Becker did come to cherish us, for a reason that had nothing to do with me personally. There were two funeral

parlors in the area, his and a larger establishment. Shortly before Warren died, we had stopped in at a wake at the other one. When we got to the car, he said, "When my heart skips that fatal beat, not this place." He said it felt as impersonal as the lobby of an empty building.

Once again following his instructions, I made the necessary arrangements with Becker, who turned out to be the antithesis of the funeral directors profiled in the bestselling book of the time that exposed the dark side of that industry, *The American Way of Death*. If it is possible to say he made that terrible time easier for all of us, he did just that. After we had used his services, the tide changed. Other people began making their funeral arrangements with him, too. "Your tragedy was the turning point in my business career," he later told me earnestly.

I thought, but didn't say, "Anything for a friend, Paul." Some fifteen years later, the kids and I were having dinner on New Year's Day at a favorite local restaurant. Paul was across the room. The waiter said that Mr. Becker wanted to offer us a drink.

"Put mine on ice," Warrie said.

"Make mine a stiff one," David ordered.

I suggested they settle for Sambuca.

Back to Mother's vigilance. Another evening, about a month after Warren died, I met some friends for a late dinner a couple of towns away. I got home around midnight to find her sitting up, waiting for me. "Mary," she said, "what are the

neighbors going to think of a girl your age walking the streets until this hour of the night?"

Mother had a stack of prayer cards for all her deceased friends and relatives. She was then seventy-six, and the list was long. It took her an hour to go through all of them each night before she went to bed. She liked to sit on a chair in the upstairs hall, where she claimed the light was better. It also was a good spot for her to overhear conversations taking place in the living room below.

Thankfully, I was surrounded by wonderful family and friends. Irene and Ken, Agnes and George Partel, and Norman and Lois Clark (not related to us) often would come over around 9:30 to share a cup of tea or glass of wine and visit with me. Mother liked to tune in to what we were saying, especially on those days when I had gone into the Tavistock office or to the studio for a recording session.

My friends and I would exchange eye signals, then one of them would ask if anything interesting was happening lately. I would start, "Well, actually, at the studio today, the most fascinating . . ." I'd then drop my voice.

Mother did not realize that even though she was out of sight, when she leaned over the banister to catch what I was saying, her shadow became more and more noticeable on the living room carpet. Finally Norman said, "We'd better cut it out, or else Nora will do a Peter Pan and come flying through the air."

One thing a new widow needs to realize is that while

friends are great, and they care and want to help you, they also have their own lives. You can't and shouldn't expect unlimited sympathy. As Annie Potters had told me, "I cried in my bed for my Bill, but people don't want to hear that all the time. They called me the 'Merry Widow.' "

Well I wasn't a "Merry Widow," but I did try to follow her example and also that of my mother. Mother was always upbeat. Granted, it's wrenching to have to go to the gatherings or parties alone, but it's a lot better than not going to them at all. You have to get used to being the third, the fifth, the seventh, the ninth, or the eleventh at the table. The important thing is that you're there. I made an arrangement with George Partel. If a group of us went out for dinner, when the check came, he would pay for me, then I'd settle with him later. It's not fair to expect the others to carry you, even if they can afford it.

Only once did someone try to hit on me. He was a guy in town whom I knew only casually. We happened to be at some big gathering, and he sidled over to me. "I know what you're missing, Mary," he murmured, adding a suggestive, "any time."

I stared at him.

"What do you think?" He smiled knowingly.

"I think Warren would not have insulted your widow," I said, and went home.

Sometimes the wives can consider a new widow a threat. I belonged to the community theater group. One night I was on the buffet line at one of their fund-raisers. A guy who was a

colossal bore got on the line behind me and started yakking away. From across the room, a penetrating voice called, "Oh, Mary, dear, just remember, that's my husband."

She should live so long that anyone else would want him, I thought.

There is nothing like a large family to keep you from having time for self-pity. In that first year, I made a total of thirteen trips to the emergency room of the local hospital with one or the other of my offspring. The nurses joked that they kept my Blue Cross number taped on the desk at the entrance. I rushed the kids in with cuts and bruises and broken arms and legs. Since almost all of the accidents occurred outside the house—on the ball field, or roller skating, or ice skating, or bike riding—at least no one could accuse me of being an abusive mother.

We got through the first Thanksgiving by having it with June and Allan and their kids. To ease the emotional wrench of Christmas, I decided I'd buy my children anything on their lists, short of a trip to the moon. I have a picture of the six of us standing in front of the tree, surrounded by games and dolls, bicycles and ice skates, a new television set. We all know you can't buy happiness. If anything is proof of that, it's that picture. The expression in everyone's eyes made Dave's "Give until it hurts" ad for United Way a comedy act.

I loved writing the scripts for *Portrait of a Patriot*. I'd always been a history buff and found the research fascinating. It was

my job to write the four-minute vignettes by starting with a question and then giving clues. It went like this:

(Bud Collier narrating.) "He was the tailor from Tennessee who became president of the United States. Do you know who he is?"

(Blast of music—dadadah!)

"This is Bud Collier with today's edition of *Portrait of a Patriot.* Our program is furnished by Grolier, publishers of *Encyclopedia Americana,* the encyclopedia that belongs in every American home.

"Our subject was born in a shack in Raleigh, North Carolina, on December 29, 1808 . . ."

At midpoint in the script, Collier asked the question, "Have you guessed who he is yet? No? Well here are more clues."

The script would end with a sentence like, "The first president to be impeached because of his defense of the constitution, he was acquitted by one vote. Our patriot today, the seventeenth president of the United States, Andrew Johnson."

(Blast of music—dadadahhh!)

"Our program has been furnished by Grolier . . ." etc., etc.

Other examples: "She was given the family tree when she was fourteen and said, 'I am nearer to the throne than I realized.' Do you know who she is?"

That was Queen Victoria.

"Crushed in the hopeless struggle, he said, 'I will fight again never, no more.' Do you know who he is?"

That was Tecumseh, the legendary chief of the Shawnee tribe.

At a recording session, I told Bud Collier that now when I went to cocktail parties, I no longer had to make small talk about the weather, that I could come up with little gems like, "Wasn't Tecumseh the one, though?" His response was that I probably wouldn't be invited to too many cocktail parties with that kind of ice breaker.

The programs had to be exactly four minutes in length. In the beginning, I didn't realize that it was very easy to snip a sentence or two off if they ran over, or add an extra beat of music if they ran a trifle short. Barry, the director, did not enlighten me. When I fearfully asked him if my programs had timed out, he would stare at me. "The first was ten seconds over. The fourth was six seconds under."

I told Liz I was sure I'd be replaced as the writer. She assured me that Barry enjoyed making people squirm.

As I was to learn, so did G. R. Tavistock.

Friends invited me to join them at the inauguration of President Lyndon Johnson in January 1965. We'd be away in Washington for just a few days. Mother urged me to go. She said it would be a nice change for me, and I knew I could use the break. I agreed but wondered if this might not be my chance to break into writing articles for *The Westwood Local*, our community newspaper. I called and offered to write a report on the inaugural. With my newfound status as a writer of

historical programs, I thought they might agree that I was exactly the person to enlighten their readers with my particular insights into the event. The editor hemmed and hawed, but then when I said that of course I wouldn't expect to be paid, he practically jumped through the phone to accept.

He promptly pulled strings to get me press passes to the various functions. Whoever dispensed them must have confused *The Westwood Local* with *The New York Times* because at the inaugural ceremony, I was seated in a prime spot and was given tickets to various events such as the most coveted Inaugural Ball. It was my first taste of "being there," which is what I called the article I wrote.

It was the first time I'd been present at an inauguration, and because everyone had expected to see John Kennedy sworn in for his second term in office, there was a palpable sadness in the air. I overheard someone say that Bobby Kennedy had made three trips to Arlington Cemetery that day. Still, Lyndon Johnson was an impressive figure as he took the oath of office and promised to launch a "Great Society." But that promise was made as protests against the Vietnam War could be heard in the distance.

I spoke to Mother every evening for those few days I was in Washington. Everything was fine, she assured me, but when I phoned to say we were getting in the car and would be home by late afternoon, I could tell that something was wrong.

I insisted she tell me what it was, pointing out that it

couldn't be worse than anything I would imagine: Dave had fallen through the ice and had to be rescued, I thought, a feat he'd managed when Warren and I were in Hawaii on the Fab-sponsored vacation. Or perhaps Patty is balking again about going to school. In the first weeks after Warren died, the nuns practically had to peel her off me in the schoolyard. She was afraid to let me out of her sight, and now I'd been away for three days.

But actually I couldn't have imagined what Mother told me: Allan, only forty-three years old and always in perfect health, had suffered a burst aneurism in his brain.

He died two weeks later, and once again we stood in stark disbelief at the family grave in Gate of Heaven cemetery and watched as his coffin was placed between those of his mother and Warren. Now there were eight fatherless Clark children, ages six to fourteen, and Ken, at thirty-three, had lost his mother and two brothers in the space of only four months.

June, Allan's widow, and I became each other's dates. We attended all the various school functions for the kids for the next twelve years until Patty, the youngest, was out of high school. We called ourselves the Dolly Sisters, after Rosie and Jenny Dolly, the showgirl sisters of the 1920s.

That spring, June and I decided to take our broods to Washington over the Easter holiday. Neither one of us was up to coloring Easter eggs or pretending that the Easter bunny was going to hip-hop merrily into our homes. Someone had

suggested an apartment rental there. "You'll love it. So comfortable. Just like home."

I don't know whose home he had in mind. We took one look at the dreary rental and paid three times the amount for rooms at the Intercontinental Hotel, which three nights later caught on fire.

We'd spent that last day sightseeing, including a visit to the White House. On the street outside, the anti–Vietnam protesters were marching and chanting. We got back to the hotel in time to let the kids have a swim in the indoor pool. Warrie, age thirteen, had just suffered three of the thirteen accidents that were visited on the family. He'd broken his wrist while roller skating, and just as that healed, he broke his arm in a fall from his bike. Dave had inadvertently sat on the arm cast while backing up from adjusting the television. Warrie had thrown a punch at him, and Dave raised his knee to protect himself.

The result was that Warrie broke his knuckles against Dave's bony knee. Since he'd have been helpless with two casts, the doctor wrapped the knuckles in thick protective bandages. The next day was April Fool's Day. When his eighth-grade teacher saw him come in with the cast on his left arm and a thick bandage on his right hand, she'd sternly told him to take the bandages off. There would be no April Fool's Day nonsense in her classroom. Warrie tried to explain, but she didn't believe him. Then when he unwrapped the bandage

and she saw his swollen knuckles, the poor woman burst into tears.

Since the injured knuckles were purely his own fault, I was getting beyond sympathy. Now they were pretty well healed, and the arm cast would be coming off in another ten days. He wanted to go swimming with the others. I finally relented, provided he agreed to stand by the side of the pool, in water only up to his waist and with his arm out of the water. For insurance, I pinned plastic around the cast. Needless to say, he got the cast wet, and it dissolved. I don't like to believe what the kids tell me I said to him—"I don't give a damn if your arm grows in crooked"—but I probably did.

That evening we watched the 6:30 national news together and saw ourselves featured in it. They had photographed the demonstrators in front of the White House, and we happened to be on the line to enter the mansion while the cameras were rolling. June and I agreed it was a good thing we weren't in Washington with hot dates. Not that we wanted them nor they us. If there's one thing that I can assure you, it is that very few men are interested in young working widows with a gang of kids to support.

That night about 3:00 A.M., a clang-clang-clang sound boomed through the hotel. I woke up. "What??????" Then thought, FIRE!

I opened the door. Smoke was filling the hallway. No one seemed to be there. We were in a two-bedroom suite. The kids

and I were all good sleepers. I wondered how long the alarm had been sounding before I woke up. I rushed to phone June, who was on the other side of the third floor. There was no answer.

I shook the kids awake and herded my little flock to the elevator. When I pushed the button, Warrie raised his now castless arm and pointed to the stairs. "You never take an elevator when there's a fire." *From the mouths of babes* . . . We rushed down the stairs. Firemen and equipment were everywhere. We found June and her three in a section of the lobby that extended beyond the building and had been deemed safe. We sat there shivering for the next hour or better, joking about our getaway vacation, until we were told to go back to the rooms.

The fire had been in a utility closet and was now out. No harm done. Everything was fine.

We were barely settled back in bed when "clang-clang-clang" again roared through the hotel. Now I was *really* worried. The fire was probably in the walls, I decided. I can't believe I actually pushed the elevator button again and once more had to be rereminded by number-one son that you always use the stairs when evacuating.

This time we weren't in the lobby long. The fire trucks, sirens blasting, returned, but in a few minutes we were assured that someone had tripped the alarm by accident. "Go to bed. Get a good night's sleep," they told us.

Right!

When we checked out the next morning, I was on line behind a man who was arguing that he didn't think he should pay for an expensive room when he'd spent most of the night shivering in the lobby or sniffing for smoke.

Ever ready to save a buck myself, I was thinking, "Go for it, pal," and praying he'd prevail.

"And it took a guest to call the fire department," the guy argued. "You people were trying to put it out on your own."

I waited for the clerk to tear up the bill. Instead, he leaned forward and dropped his voice to a stage whisper. "Sir, I'm going to share something with you. I worked in a hotel in Boston where *three floors were in flames* before the management sent for the fire department."

That was such a stunning lie that the guy gave up arguing. He paid. I paid. June paid. You can't win 'em all.

They used to say about President Herbert Hoover that he had so keen a memory for names and faces that he could kiss a baby and thirty years later shake the hand of the voter and address him by name.

Obviously, that's an exaggeration, but there is no doubt that some of us never forget a name or face, while others are genetically hopeless at either. I belong to the second group. I've always maintained that if I met my mother in a place where I didn't expect to find her, and she was wearing a new hat, I'd introduce myself to her.

Now that I was going into New York regularly and meet-

ing a host of new people, I was determined to remedy that deficit.

June had a different problem to overcome. She was terribly shy about speaking in public, but she loved politics, was active in the Republican party, and knew that she wanted to run for office someday. Obviously, in order to do that, she needed to be able to overcome her shyness.

We both noticed an ad in the paper for the Dale Carnegie course in self-improvement, meeting one night a week for fourteen weeks. Dale Carnegie, a motivational lecturer and author, had written one of the bestselling books of all time, *How to Win Friends and Influence People.* According to the ad, by signing up for the course, we would become more outgoing and more successful. The course also promised to improve our memories so that we would almost never again forget someone's name. That promise turned me on.

June and I elected to go for it and with some trepidation attended the first session. There were about fifteen of us in the class. The instructor introduced himself. "My name is Fred Vest," he said, smiling. "Now I want you all to introduce yourselves to me, and then I will demonstrate to you how really easy it is to commit names to memory."

We dutifully obeyed. He repeated our names, paused, and then greeted us by name, without a moment's hesitation. "Your names have been committed to my memory," he said. "I will never forget any of you. Now let me explain how easy it is for you to be proficient in the same way."

He cleared his throat. "You notice how I repeated each of your names when you introduced yourselves. You must always do that. Then, looking directly at the other person, you must repeat his name twice, picturing it written in bronze across the sky. At the same time, you must associate the name of the person you are meeting with something about him or her that will become your word association that will trigger your memory when you meet him again. For example, my name is Vest. Fred Vest. I am vested with authority in this class. As you write my name in bronze across the sky, keep the thought that I am vested with authority."

Vest, I thought. He's vested with authority. I had his name down pat. I was sure of it. Frank Vest. For the next thirteen weeks I called him Frank and either he didn't notice or didn't care.

There was a distinct emphasis in the course on learning to raise the tone level of our voice, and therefore raising the tone level of the people around us. The idea was that when you woke up in the morning, even if things weren't going right, if you were worried about anything or upset about anything, if you got out of bed moody or grouchy or depressed, you would undoubtedly pass those vibes on to everyone you contacted. Your husband or your wife and kids, or the guy at the newspaper stand, or your fellow employees—you could lower their tone levels through your woebegone demeanor or curt greeting.

On the other hand, if you acted cheerful and optimistic and smiling, and had a spring in your step, you'd be passing around good vibrations that would influence everyone you greeted. In turn, they would respond in a cheery way to you, and then they would be influencing the people they greeted, buoyed as they had been by your sunny demeanor.

It made sense to me. All through twelve years of Catholic school, I had been taught to follow the example of St. Francis, and to be an instrument of peace. One sweet elderly nun had warned us that sometime someone might be very rude or unkind to us but that we should never respond in kind. She explained that maybe that poor, dear person had just received terrible news, perhaps about the grave illness of someone he or she loved very much, and had never intended to offend us. Then, too, there was the possibility that the poor, troubled soul who had unwittingly offended us had done so because he or she wasn't feeling well, or maybe was even very ill and about to die. Wouldn't it be a terrible burden for our conscience if that person suffered a heart attack a moment after we had lashed out at him or her, leaving us to know that our unkind words were the last words that sweet, troubled soul ever heard on this earth?

That possibility had always worried me. I'm sure my father's sudden death had a lot to do with it, but I have always had a hard time even telling someone that his big, fat foot was resting on my sore toe. To me, the advice about cheering up

the world was simply an extension of everything I'd been taught, but at the Dale Carnegie course, they added a new wrinkle on how to go about it.

The trick, we were told, was that upon awakening, we should sit up in bed, throw out our arms, and shout, "Good morning, day!" Up would go our tone level. Guaranteed. We practiced in class.

The following Saturday, I decided to give it a whirl. Warren had been gone for nine months, and I woke up feeling snake low. Weekends always were harder, because all the men in the neighborhood were around, and their presence emphasized the fact that Warren was gone and that I was alone. I sat up, threw out my arms, and bellowed, "Good morning, day!"

My hand hit something. That something was the tray with a pot of coffee, orange juice, and an English muffin that the kids had laid on the bed. On Saturday mornings, they would do that, then get their own juice or cocoa, come back upstairs and get into bed with me. I called it our "souls at sea" get-together. Pat and Carol would be propped against the headboard to my left and right, while the other three sat cross-legged at my feet. The whole effect kind of resembled a crowded lifeboat.

Following the advice of an article I'd read, I'd changed the décor of the bedroom to give it a different look, *my* room not *our* room. Now orange juice and coffee and melted butter were dripping down the sides of the new bedspread and onto the new carpet.

With Carol, in one of our modeling shots.

I ran for a towel, began to sop up the mess, and had a lot of words to mutter under my breath, no three of which were "Good morning, day."

Actually, June and I were apt Dale Carnegie students and both won awards at the graduation ceremony. The award was a pencil with the reason for the honor printed on the side. June's pencil read, "First in personal experience," honoring her final speech at the course. Mine read, "First in human relations." I absolutely forget what speech I gave to deserve that singular honor, but one night in the Port Authority Bus Terminal in Manhattan, I was jotting down a phone number, and a guy a few feet away began smiling suggestively at me.

I couldn't figure him out until I realized that I was using my Dale Carnegie pencil, which announced that I'd won first prize in human relations. Maybe he thought I was advertising.

It was on graduation night that I realized I'd been calling the instructor by the wrong name and humbly accepted the fact that I wasn't going to become a second Herbert Hoover in the memory department. On the other hand, June went on to become a very effective speaker and was elected a freeholder in Bergen County, a position she held for years.

My first bona-fide date was with a fellow student from the course. He was on temporary assignment in the area with his company, and I think he signed up for the course simply to pass the time. Alas, I don't remember his name. He was a

pleasant-looking, quiet guy in his early fifties, and when he invited me to have dinner with him the following Friday night, I thought, Why not? It would be a welcome change from always being the extra woman at the table.

I'd been at the Tavistock office all that day. I got caught in traffic, and when I arrived home, I was only ten minutes ahead of the time he was expected. The kids had already eaten, and before I rushed upstairs to shower and change, I reminded them I was having dinner with a friend, that they should invite him in when he arrived and make him feel welcome.

They hadn't really paid attention to the fact that I was going out, but now I was peppered with questions: "Who is he?"

"Do we know him?"

"Is Aunt June going with you?"

It was obvious they were not happy with the thought that I was going out by myself with a strange man.

Marilyn, now fourteen, came upstairs about fifteen minutes later as I was putting on makeup. "Your father's here," she announced. "He's very big on hurricanes. That's all he's been talking about since he walked in the door."

When I got downstairs, my fellow Dale Carnegie student was sitting in the wing chair, across from the couch. My five offspring were lined up and gazing at him, their expressions polite, but bored.

"But it wasn't as bad as the hurricane that hit Puerto Rico ten years ago," he was saying.

He knew I had children. Knowing about them and seeing them in the flesh, however, were two different matters. Anyhow, if the Dale Carnegie course had helped him to develop a winning personality, I couldn't find it that evening, nor did he notice mine. When he dropped me off at home at ten o'clock, the kids were in the den watching television.

They looked up to see my reaction to my date. I realized that maybe they'd been worried about it. I said, "The hurricane in Puerto Rico didn't hold a candle to the one in Timbuktu."

"What a jerk," was their relieved comment.

That very nice man wasn't a jerk, but they didn't want any man to become part of their lives and neither did I. If there was one thing I was absolutely certain wouldn't happen, it was that I'd get involved with anyone. There were two good reasons for that certainty. The first was that it's hard enough for the natural parent to raise children. You would willingly give your life for them, but on the other hand there are times you want to send one or the other of them into orbit.

I knew immediately that I'd never take the chance of having my children in the position of having a stepfather who might not get along with all of them. I was certain that it would be better for them to grow up with the memory of a father they knew had loved them dearly and equally.

The second reason was that I wanted to give them a good education. I wanted them to go to fine colleges and to gradu-

ate school if they were so inclined. To achieve that goal, I had to work. I didn't want any man to be in the position of dictating where my children would be educated.

Suppose someone had come along who was reasonably successful and wanted me to be available to be a stay-at-home wife? That would make me totally dependent on someone else's generosity, and I wasn't about to be placed in that position.

That doesn't mean that even in that first year I didn't hope that someday when the kids were grown up I'd meet someone I could care about. I missed being married. I missed the companionship, the closeness, the friendship that is the essence of a good marriage. In my diary I wrote, "The world goes two by two."

Warrie graduated from the eighth grade in June. There was a party for the graduates, and he invited one of the girls in his class. He asked me to drive them. When we got in the car, he climbed into the backseat. "When we pick her up, don't say anything, Mom, just drive, okay?"

On the way to his friend's house, I felt a sudden sense of panic. I realized a new chapter was beginning. I was dealing with a son who was growing up fast, who was on his first date. How do you raise adolescent boys without a father? Would he put his arm around the girl? Would he kiss her good night? What about the facts of life? How much did he know?

Warrie interrupted my reverie. "It's this house." He got out of the car. "Now, remember, just drive, okay?"

"Sure."

A moment later he returned, escorting a pretty thirteen year old with bouncy golden hair and a great figure. She nodded to me shyly. I nodded back, keeping my promise to say nothing. They got into the backseat.

"You know what?" she asked Warrie.

She sounded seductive. I strained to hear what she was about to tell him.

"What?" Warrie asked.

"My dog threw up today."

"Oh, gee, that's too bad."

I relaxed. If that was the level of conversation, for the present, at least, I didn't have to worry about budding teenage romances.

It wasn't hard to keep busy. I was given a second radio series to write, *The Alcoa News Calendar*. The format was current events–type news followed by a safety hint from the FBI. The Alcoa company was one of the sponsors of the then popular television series *The FBI*, and the safety hint served as a daily plug for the series.

I based what I wrote on information sent to me by an FBI agent, who had to approve every word before it was aired. The safety hints went like this:

"If you're going shopping and the parking area is crowded,

be sure to park your car in a well-lighted area. However, if you ever feel you're being followed, run to the nearest well-lighted house and ring the bell. If on the other hand, you feel you are going to be cornered, take off your shoe, hold it by the toe, and aim the heel at the bridge of the nose of your attacker."

Another one began, "If you're alone in the house and hear footsteps on the stairs . . ."

I'd always honestly claimed that I'd never been nervous anywhere, but after I'd been writing that series for a while, I found my eyes darting for a potential predator as I got in my car, soaked in my tub, or awakened to a strange sound in the night.

I took on a third series, *The Art of Gift-Giving*, furnished by S&H Green Stamps. S&H had a slogan for the stamps: "For all your gift-giving needs, even for the gift you want just for yourself."

The format was for me to write about famous gifts in history, poignant gifts, funny gifts, gifts that changed the course of a life, gifts that led to another career. Bess Myerson was the celebrity narrator for this series. Like the *Portrait of a Patriot* series, it began with a question. Example: "Do you know about the gift that was turned against the giver?"

That program was about George III, America's last king. Upon learning that his American colonists were getting restive, he sent over a statue of himself on horseback as a gift. When the Revolution broke out, the colonists melted it down and used it for bullets.

Or: "Do you know about the gift Queen Victoria gave her grandson?"

Victoria wrote in her diary that her grandson, Willie, the future Kaiser Wilhelm, was a tiresome little boy, but when he turned twenty-one, her birthday present to him was Mount Kilimanjaro.

I enjoyed doing the research necessary for all the series, but the days began to feel as though there weren't enough hours in them.

The goal at the G. R. Tavistock office was to keep the series on the air. The longer they ran, the more profitable they were, because the start-up costs were being amortized. That was why whenever a series was up for renewal, it was crisis time. Everyone was dedicated to making that renewal happen. When a series was canceled, the wrath of G.R. descended upon the office.

Gordon Tavistock was a strikingly handsome man with a powerful personality. If you didn't work for him, you'd find him charming. Working for him, however, was another kettle of fish. That first year I was a freelance writer, and as long as my scripts were good and on time, all was well. But then he sent word that I was needed in the office to have regular client contact and to go out on sales calls to advertising agencies and sponsors. He said that I could continue to write my current three series on the side.

The change in duties meant commuting into New York

every morning and not getting home until 6:30 at night. Mother was absolutely against the idea. "Stay home and mind your children, Mary," she urged. But I really didn't have a choice. I couldn't make even half the money somewhere else, and I didn't want my children to be "gee whiz" kids who couldn't attend the schools their friends were attending, or who couldn't even consider going on school trips because there wouldn't be money to send them. Being present in the office also meant that I could have a chance to be the writer of a new series if any of the ones I was working on were canceled, and that was terribly important.

I was aware that churning out the scripts was helping me to become a better all-around writer. When you have to tell a story in four minutes less product credit lines, you learn to write succinctly. I didn't realize at the time that I was in training to be a suspense writer, in a genre where every word has to move the action forward.

When the first anniversary of Warren's death came around, a new phase of my life began—carpooling into New York with my brother-in-law Ken and Clem Weber, whose wife, Rose, was one of my closest friends. When you're commuting to business with men, it's not like going out for a leisurely lunch with the girls. You have to be precisely on time when the car pulls into the driveway to pick you up.

Mornings became a scramble. The rushed routine went something as follows: Wake the kids up at quarter of seven.

Get breakfast on the table. Skinny as the boys were, they were hearty breakfast eaters. Carol had a hard time waking up. I practically had to dress her, then shake her awake at the table. Patty, still loath to go to school, claimed to have a stomachache every day.

"You're going to school," I'd say firmly.

"My stomach *really* hurts."

"You're going to school, Pat."

Marilyn, now a sophomore in high school, seemed always to be looking for her homework or lunch bag as her carpool waited outside.

By twenty of eight, they were on their way. At quarter of eight, Clem, with Ken next to him in the front seat, pulled into my driveway, and I ran to the car. As often as not, my hair was still up, my makeup and jewelry at the bottom of my purse, and sometimes my stockings still needed to be pulled on. The guys said it was indecent to look into the backseat until we reached the George Washington Bridge because I was still dressing. Clem's wife, Rose, said, "It's a good thing I know you so well, Mary. Otherwise I'd be wondering why I sometimes find a pink curler or a lipstick in the back of my husband's car."

Portrait of a Patriot was my first and favorite series. Naturally it was necessary to do at least one program each on all the presidents. I had deliberately put off writing about George Washington because I considered him abysmally dull. The idiotic stories I had heard about him, such as "Father, I cannot

tell a lie. I chopped down the cherry tree," had given me the impression that he was a world-class nerd. I had read also that he had been in love with his best friend's wife, and married Martha, an older, wealthy woman, for her money. The picture of the two of them, obviously mature, with young children at their feet, reinforced that nerdy impression. Then, too, he appeared so grim in all the portraits. Did he ever smile? I wondered.

Nonetheless, I had to write about him for the series, so I began to do research on him. The more I read, the more I realized how badly I had misjudged him. Washington was a towering and fascinating figure. Over six feet three at a time when most men were five feet seven or less, he stood literally head and shoulders above his peers. To my astonishment, I learned that he was considered the best dancer in the colony of Virginia. He also was a superb rider, so much so that the Indians paid him their highest compliment: "He walks and rides his horse like an Indian." At twenty-six, he became a hero of the French and Indian War. At age sixteen, he had developed a huge crush on the so-called love of his life, eighteen-year-old Sally Carey Fairfax. They remained lifelong friends, but Martha was the true love of his life. Yes, she was older, but only eight months older—twenty-seven to his twenty-six—when they married.

Like Lady Bird Johnson, Martha was never called by her given name. When she was little, her father had decreed that Martha was much too formidable a name for such a tiny girl

and nicknamed her Patsy. George called her "My dearest Patsy." She went through the British lines to join him in Boston. She spent the winter in Valley Forge with him.

I wrote a number of scripts about George and Martha Washington, and as I did, an idea began to form in my head. I missed the printed word. I enjoyed writing the radio programs, but they vanished after they'd been aired. On the other hand, I could pick up a magazine that was eight or nine years old and still see my story in print. I wanted to be in print again.

My agent, Pat Myrer, had been urging me to write a novel. "There's no market for short stories," she reminded me.

I started thinking about writing a novel about George Washington, one in which the facts and events would be historically accurate, one that would be written from his viewpoint. The seed began to grow. But when would I find the time to do it? There was only one answer: I'd have to get up at five o'clock and work until quarter of seven, when I got the kids up for school.

The first few mornings of the new routine were tough. When the alarm went off, my inclination was to slap my finger on it and close my eyes. But it wasn't that hard to get used to rising early. And once I was at the kitchen table with the typewriter in place and a cup of coffee at my elbow, it was sheer bliss to be able to work, knowing that the phone wasn't going to ring, that one of the children wouldn't need something immediately.

I started to outline the book. I made a couple of flying trips to Mount Vernon. I immersed myself in nonfiction books about G.W. I began the first chapter. I bumped into Pat Myrer on Park Avenue. "Write," she urged me.

"I'm writing a novel," I said happily.

"Marvelous. What about?"

"George Washington."

Seeing Pat's stunned expression, I forged ahead, gushing about the great love story I would tell about George and Martha.

Pat interrupted me. "Love story between those two? Mary, with those wooden teeth, the only thing George ever gave Martha was splinters."

But it was an itch I had to scratch. I had to write that book. I knew I was on my way to becoming a novelist.

TWELVE

I had flown with Pan Am for a year, but my buddy, Joan Murchison, with whom I'd left Remington Rand to become a stewardess, stayed with the airline for seven years. Then she married a marvelous British war hero, Col. Richard Broad, whom she'd met on one of her trips. When Carol was born, she brought him to visit me in St. Vincent's Hospital. They made a gorgeous couple. She was petite and blond; Richard was tall and elegant. He'd been an aide to King George VI. When World War II broke out, he was captured and held in a prisoner of war camp in Spain. Sentenced to be shot, he managed to escape with seven of his men. For the next year, they worked their way through occupied France until they finally managed to get back to England. One winter had been spent in the attic of a convent. His group became known as "Snow White and the Seven Dwarfs."

When Joan brought him back to the hospital a second

time, I said, "Murch, for the love of heaven, that poor man has better things to do with his time in New York than twiddle his thumbs on a maternity floor."

She smiled. "Mary, he's special."

Richard was indeed special. At that time he was director of a diamond company and was living in Johannesburg. That's where he and Joan were married. She got back to the States several times a year to visit her mother in Illinois and always spent a few days in New York to catch up with her close friends.

A couple of months after I started working fulltime, I met her at the airport, and we drove into Manhattan. We stopped at a store where she needed to pick up something she had ordered. I waited in the car. When she came back a few minutes later, I was asleep. That was the moment when I realized I needed some household help. I was simply exhausted.

Mother was nearly seventy-eight. She suffered from arthritis, and it was getting harder and harder for her to get around. The kids were starting dinner before I got home, but on several occasions, a neighbor who was a volunteer fireman had to come running over with his fire extinguisher to put out a fire in the oven. Somehow the concept of not putting chops an inch from the flame never did register with my little chefs. We needed help.

One of Tavistock's out-of-town clients heard that I was fishing around for a live-in housekeeper and called me. He had a friend in her late fifties who wanted to live in the New

York area, and she'd worked as a housekeeper. Was I interested? Sight unseen, I took her on. Her name was Peg, and she turned out to be a nice person and a good cook. Also, the driving problem with getting the kids back and forth to activities was solved.

Our arrangement was that she would work from Monday till Friday. The downside was that even though she had the weekend off, she seldom took advantage of it. She stayed around the house on weekends, neither fish nor fowl, helping occasionally, but not really working. And when she did pitch in, she'd take on a slightly martyred expression. Even though we had moved to a larger house in town the year before Warren died, the place wasn't very roomy. I longed for Peg to disappear on Friday evening and return Monday morning. I wanted time to be alone with my family.

Then out of the blue, I'd sometimes find a note taped to the refrigerator, telling me she'd decided to take a couple of days off. It took a while before it dawned on me that when Peg disappeared, the client who had suggested her to me was in town. I wondered if there was anything going on. I was uncomfortable with the idea of her discussing my household with a client.

Another problem was that I learned that while the kids were in school, Peg was parking my unmistakable bright yellow, nine-passenger station wagon outside the local bar, where she was moonlighting by playing piano for the afternoon

drinkers. I hoped that the people in our little town didn't think that *I* was the one who had parked it there.

In a lot of ways she was a big help, but when, after a year and a half, she said that she thought it was time to move on, I didn't shed any tears. She interviewed for and was offered a job as cook working for David Sarnoff, the powerful media giant. His cook had gone to work for Jackie Kennedy Onassis. I told my friends that I was only two kitchens away from Jackie, but ultimately Peg wisely decided that she'd be biting off more than she could chew to be responsible for preparing gourmet dinner parties for up to twelve people.

Instead she moved to California with the family of a television personality. She wrote to tell me that she had become best friends with Florence Aadland, who had written that great first line, "I don't care what anyone says. My baby was a virgin when she met Errol Flynn."

G.R. had decided that I'd make a good salesman for the Gordon R. Tavistock radio programming plan. Since that task could earn me a commission on any shows I sold, I was happy to give it a whirl. My only selling experience had been brief and came during my Remington Rand years: I'd had a Saturday job at Lord & Taylor selling coats. The pay had been five dollars a day, but the real perk was the 30 percent employee discount. I loved clothes, and that was a good way to acquire a wardrobe. I'd keep an eye on a dress or suit that I

wanted, sure that at some point it would be reduced, then track it until the final reduction and buy it with my 30 percent discount.

I quickly learned that there was a big difference between selling winter coats and getting the advertising executives to sign up for a minimum of fifteen thousand dollars for radio programming. I needed all my Dale Carnegie "win friends and influence people" know-how to get up the nerve to phone an account executive and persuade him to give me an appointment. But I started to fill my appointment book.

My first sale seemed to be an easy one. I had an appointment at J. Walter Thompson, one of the world's leading advertising agencies. It was also the one for which I had a tender feeling—it was the agency that had hired my son Dave to do the *Peanuts* commercials for Ford's Falcon station wagon, in which he'd been the voice of Linus for four years.

The account executive I saw there couldn't have been more charming. The kind of publicity I was offering sounded great. He'd be delighted to have his product on radio. Come back with a contract.

Flushed with success, I returned to the office and announced I had made my first sale. "Great!" "Terrific!" "Wonderful!" Then someone asked me what product the agency wanted to publicize.

"Preparation H."

The smiles faded. I was told that there was no way a highly

personal product like Preparation H could be mentioned on the airways. "No wonder the account executive jumped through hoops when he thought he could get a whole series publicizing his product's soothing qualities," I was told. "He'd have been promoted on the spot if he could put that one over." In other words, I not only didn't have the sale, but I ended up looking like an idiot for even proposing the possibility of one.

Now, when I hear the advertisements for the most intimate products on radio or see them on television, I realize what a quaintly innocent world we lived in less than four decades ago, when the fact that you might suffer from hemorrhoids could not be mentioned on the air. It's progress of a sort, I guess.

But I did succeed in opening an account with the Nestlé Company. This time the product was chocolate chip cookies, and no one, but *no one,* had any objection to talking about them anywhere, anytime.

The program was called *The Wonderful World of Food.* Betsy Palmer was the celebrity hostess. That began my friendship with Betsy that has endured all these years. She's a great gal, a wonderful narrator, and a terrific actress. The success of that series led to four more with Nestlé.

In the frequent absences of Tavistock, Frank Reeves ran the office. More than that, he was the true heart and soul of the business. He was the kind of person who could sell ice to

Eskimos and knew how to make lifelong friends of clients. He kept programs on the air long after anyone else would have lost them. When I went to work for Tavistock, Frank's wife, Happy, was an invalid. I admired the way that he went straight home after work, taking the train to Long Island. He had a host of friends and constantly received invitations to dinners and parties, but his answer was always the same: "Can't make it. I have to get home to Happy."

Not realizing that she was violently allergic to penicillin, Happy had been given a penicillin injection that brought on a stroke. Then she had a second stroke in 1965, the same week that Warren's brother Allan died. After that, totally bedridden, she lived only another two years.

In addition to being a good husband and boss, Frank was the one responsible for introducing me to Cape Cod. A native of Boston, he had spent all his summers on the Cape. The summer after losing his wife, he rented a house in the town of Dennis and invited five of us from the office to spend a weekend there.

For some reason I'd always been intrigued with Cape Cod. When I was growing up, the women's magazines had stories about the people who summered on the Cape and whose husbands took the train up for weekends. I considered them an exalted lot and wondered how it would be to live in the place where the Pilgrims first lived when they came over on the *Mayflower*. The five of us from the office flew up on a Friday

in July. Incredibly, it only cost sixteen dollars for the flight. Today the same trip—in what I suspect may be the same plane—costs well over two hundred dollars, one way.

The minute I got off the plane, I felt as though I'd come home. I had the most extraordinary sensation of being in a place that I knew intimately. I don't believe in reincarnation, but I do wonder sometimes if it isn't possible that we inherit memory. If we can look exactly like someone who lived hundreds of years ago, if we inherit that person's particular gift or talent, his or her allergies, isn't it possible that we can also inherit some awareness that comes from a memory base? I don't think there are many people who haven't at some time, some place had a sense of déjà vu: *This is familiar but I don't know why.*

Anyhow, that was the response I felt when I got off the plane in Hyannis in July 1968. Déjà vu. Familiarity. Returning home. I've never lost that feeling whenever I go there.

I've been summering at the Cape ever since. A month after that first visit, I returned to the Cape with the four younger kids. Marilyn had a summer job and wanted to stay home with my mother. I had a number of friends in the Dennis area, so I rented two cabins in a motel unit on Route 6A in East Dennis, where I unwittingly succeeded in terrifying two elderly residents who were luckless enough to be staying in the cabin adjacent to one of ours.

The cabins were small. Carol had a girlfriend, Beth, with

her. I stayed in one of the cabins with them and at night sent Patty to sleep with the boys in their unit. They were situated up an incline and a little to the left. The arrangement was that I'd give the boys a few minutes to change for bed, then Patty would join them.

We'd been out for dinner and miniature golf, so it was nearly eleven o'clock when we got back to the motel. The walls were paper thin, so I cautioned Carol and Beth to keep the television down to a whisper. I took Patty, bundled in her pajamas and robe and holding her tattered security blanket, outside. Warrie waved to us from the boys' cabin, and Patty started up the incline. I watched until she joined Warrie, and he closed the door, then I turned back and realized that the television was blasting. I flung open the door of the cabin, cried, "Are you two trying to wake up the dead?" and rushed over to the television to turn it off.

Then I turned around. What I had not realized was that in watching Pat go up the incline, I had been moving to the right. I was now standing in the cabin next to ours. Staring at me from the pullout bed was an elderly couple, their eyes large with terror, their mouths open. I swear even their teeth, soaking in glasses on either side of the bed, began chattering.

"I'm sorry . . . I'm so sorry . . ." Frantically I tried to turn on the television and tune it to the program they'd been watching, but I only succeeded in getting a snow-filled screen and screeching static. With a final mumbled apology, I rushed out of the cabin and went next door where I belonged. Carol

and Beth had heard everything through the thin walls and were collapsed in fits of giggling.

The next morning at 6:00 A.M., the car in front of the next cabin pulled out. The elderly couple had fled. I hope they came back. I would hate to think that I had driven them from Cape Cod forever.

THIRTEEN

*I*t had been nearly three years since Warren's death, but Patty was still stealing into my room at night and then slipping away early in the morning so the big kids wouldn't think she was a baby. That was why when June bought a dog for her kids and Pat asked if we could get one too. I thought it would be a good idea. Growing up, Johnny and I had always been allergic to most animals, but poodles don't shed, and I knew I wouldn't have a problem with one of them.

I was working on my book about George Washington, and we lived in Washington Township. That was how our miniature poodle came to be named Sir George the First of Washington Township. *"Georgy Porgy, puddin' and pie, kissed the girls and made them cry."* That old nursery rhyme inspired us to call our newcomer Porgy. We got him when he was only a few weeks old, and he slept in a shoebox next to Patty's bed.

After his arrival, she no longer made nocturnal visits to my room. While I was very pleased that the addition of Porgy to the household brought some comfort to the kids, especially Patty, he occasionally caused a crisis.

One evening when I arrived home, Patty frantically told me that Porgy had just run out the back door and taken off. I immediately got in the car and began to drive slowly through my darkened neighborhood.

A couple of tense hours later, I spotted him trotting merrily down the block and stopped the car.

"Get in," I snarled.

Obediently, he hopped in beside me.

All the way home, I ranted at him about his escapade. He followed me into the house, and in the brightness of the kitchen, I realized to my horror that the dog was not Porgy. I was a dognapper and pictured myself behind bars.

I rushed him back into the car and raced the several blocks to where I had found him. As I shoved him out of the car, I heard a worried voice yelling, "Charley, Charley . . ." His tail wagging, he bounded away.

A few minutes after I got home, a happy bark from outside the kitchen door announced Porgy's triumphant return. We later learned that he had returned from a hot date with a lady poodle who had moved in around the corner.

My mother was turning eighty. In the last years, her friends had been celebrating their fiftieth wedding anniversaries. She,

My mother, Nora, on her eightieth birthday.

of course, had been widowed for some twenty-seven years. I decided that since she couldn't have an anniversary bash, I was going to throw her an eightieth birthday party. At first I considered making it a surprise, but then I decided that planning is half the fun. I told her what I had in mind, overcame her objections that it would cost too much, and suggested that she start making out a list of the people she wanted to invite.

She had suffered from arthritis ever since she was twenty. It was indicative of her whole approach to life that she contracted it dancing barefoot in the snow in Central Park when she was nineteen. As she aged, it spread to her knees and legs, her feet and hands, and finally to her back. Her feet were affected the worst, and she literally walked to heaven on those painful appendages, so swollen and sore that she could hardly endure her weight on them. She probably would have been confined to a wheelchair, were it not for the fact that her need to do for other people was so great that she kept pushing herself, forcing activity on those aching joints, willing them to function.

The planning for her party gave her a new lease on life. After listing the obvious guests—her remaining two sisters, nieces and nephews, and longtime friends like Annie Potters—she began looking up addresses of cousins and cronies who had drifted out of our regular orbit. For the occasion, our friend George Partel built a platform, and on it we placed a wing chair draped in velvet and surrounded by flow-

ers. On her eightieth birthday, we made Mother "Queen for a Day."

My brother Johnny had a sparkle in his eye that I had not seen for a long time. The baby's death and then the breakup of his marriage had been devastating for him. He had begun dating a woman named Connie, and I suspected he might be getting serious.

The party started at three in the afternoon because I was sure that Mother and the other old girls would get tired early. I should have known better. Twelve hours later, my contemporaries and I sat limply in the den while Mother and her peers stood around the piano, happily singing "Sweet Molly Malone."

That night I marveled at Mother. Wearing her best beige lace dress, her silver hair framing her almost unlined face, her blue eyes sparkling, she was obviously having the time of her life. Before that party finally ended, she had cast her cane aside, locked arms with the remaining "Bungalow Girls"— friends from Rockaway Beach, circa 1912—and led a spirited if limited version of the Rockettes chorus line.

She was to live for another year and a half, a period during which her health failed drastically. I was always sorry that God hadn't called her right after that party. Instead of suffering, she'd have gone out on a high note.

Mother loved to go home to her quiet Bronx apartment for weekends. One Saturday she phoned. "Mary," she said, "I think John is married. What are we going to do about it?"

"Throw a shower for him?" I suggested.

"Mary, you know what I mean."

I did. Johnny was dating, but he was divorced and in Mother's Catholic eyes not free to marry. "Mother, you'll have no peace unless you call up Johnny and ask him point blank if he's married," I said.

Deciding it was the only thing to do, she phoned him. "John," she began, "I have a question to ask you."

He told me later that he knew immediately what was coming.

"John, are you married?"

"Yes, Mother, I'm married."

"Were you married by a priest within the faith?"

"No, Mother, but the judge who married us is very active in the Knights of Columbus."

Mother's response was to laugh. "Congratulations. I hope you'll both be very happy." She was always a good sport and had long ago learned to accept what couldn't be changed.

I would go out occasionally on dates. Someone I met at a Mystery Writers meeting began to show interest in me. There had been a short-lived television series in which the main character, named Stanley Beamish, could fly. The kids decided my admirer was a look-alike for Stanley Beamish. When he called, instead of telling me who was on the phone, they would start flapping their arms. He didn't last as long as the failed TV show.

From time to time, people tried to set me up with their

friends. One day someone from town showed up on my doorstep. "Mary," he demanded, "how old are you?"

I was so surprised I blurted out the exact truth.

Satisfied, he nodded. "That's what I thought. I have someone I want you to meet. He's an engineer who works for our company. He makes fourteen thousand a year. There's just one problem. He's very cranky."

"For fifty thousand a year, I'll look at a crank," I told this self-made Dolly Levi. "For fourteen thousand, he has to be Smiling Jack."

I never did meet the engineer.

At work, Frank and I had become a team. I would open up a potential new account, and he would come in to close the deal. We regularly took clients and our celebrity hosts to lunch and sometimes to dinner and the theater. Then we'd have a quick cup of coffee and I'd go home to New Jersey and he to Long Island.

He was very fond of me—I knew that. I also knew that he was terrified of the fact that I had five children. What he never understood was that I had no plans to marry anyone. Nevertheless, he was always on guard about appearing interested in me. The only time his guard slipped was when he was feeling sentimental, usually following a pleasant dinner. After his elderly parents died, he had had his mother's diamonds inserted into his father's signet ring. On three or four occasions, in front of clients or friends, he would take off "Dad's ring," as

we called it, slip it on my finger, and announce to one and all that we were engaged.

The next morning at work, I would give him the ring back and assure him that we weren't engaged. I knew that he must have awakened shivering with fear that the five kids, Porgy the poodle, and I would arrive at his doorstep. "Dad's ring" became a long-standing joke among our friends. "Have you given Mary 'Dad's ring' lately, Frank?" was a question that came up from time to time.

We've remained devoted friends through the years, and one Christmas Eve he handed me a brown paper bag. "Dad's ring," he said, "I want you to have it. No strings attached."

During that period of my life, one bright interlude that occurred every year and a half or so was that I'd steal a week to go to England and visit my old friend Joan and her husband, Richard. They had moved to the village of Branscombe, in Devon, and were living in a former coast guard station, called "The Lookout," which they had converted to a magnificent country home. High on a hill overlooking the English Channel and situated on five hundred acres, it was balm to my soul to visit there.

Joan, who had been afraid of horses when she was young, had become a superb horsewoman. Richard kept a stable and rode every morning, and she wisely had thrown herself into sharing his passion, becoming an expert jumper when they rode to hounds. I'd taken a few lessons along the way, and riding was something I'd always wanted to do. Over there, I was

assigned one of the gentle horses and would go out with them. Cantering on the British countryside beside the English Channel, I felt a long way from the Bronx.

I remember the time I urged them to come over and spend Thanksgiving with us. "You don't have Thanksgiving here, Richard," I reminded him.

"Oh, but we do, Mary," he said. "You must remember, your Fourth of July is our Thanksgiving."

In 1968, after three years of getting up to write at 5:00 A.M., I finished my book on George and Martha Washington. I entitled it *Aspire to the Heavens* because that had been the family motto of Mary Ball Washington, George's mother. It is, of course, one of the truly terrible titles of all time. When it was published a year later, the few bookstores it slithered into placed it in the "spiritual" section, between the Bible and Norman Vincent Peale. The clerks thought it was a prayer book.

But it *was* published, and that's what mattered most. I had written a book, and I have to say I thought it was good. Alas, not only the title conspired to make sure that it remained one of the great secrets of 1969, the publishing house was sold just as the book came out, and as a result there was not one iota of publicity to help enlighten the world that my first book was available. For some reason, though, it did manage to find its way into a bookstore near our office. One day, three or four of us passed that bookstore on the way to lunch.

I stopped, staring in shock: a copy of *Aspire to the Heavens*

was in the window. I pointed it out to my fellow Tavistockites. "Front and center," I boasted.

When we returned from lunch, the book was missing from the window. "Snapped up!" I said.

At five o'clock the same group again passed the bookstore window. A copy of *Aspire to the Heavens* was again in place.

"Whoever bought it returned it," one of the guys suggested.

I had received a total of fifteen hundred dollars less 10 percent commission for three years' work. I had no way of knowing that over three decades later the book would be discovered by a descendant of the Washington family and go on the bestseller list under its new and more appropriate title, *Mount Vernon Love Story*.

I did know that I considered the book a triumph. And I also knew that I had what it took to actually write a book. Now I wanted to try to write a book that would sell. Marilyn was a freshman at Catholic University. Warren was about to graduate from high school and was enrolled in Villanova University. I needed to make more money.

I have a hot tip I offer people who say to me, "I know I can write. I'm sure I can write. I just don't know what to write." I tell them to turn around and look at their bookshelves. What do they like to read? Oh sure, we are all to some degree eclectic readers, but what do we grab when we're running for a plane or train? What do we curl up with when we're tired at

the end of the day and want to just lose ourselves in a book? Is it a classic, a biography, mystery/suspense, science fiction or romance? Whatever your favorite reading is may well indicate where your literary pot of gold is waiting.

I looked at my bookshelves and realized that, from the time I was six years old, I'd loved to read suspense. The Judy Bolton and Nancy Drew series, then Agatha Christie, Josephine Tey, Ngaio Marsh, Charlotte Armstrong, Mignon G. Eberhart, Rex Stout, John D. MacDonald—the list went on and on.

More than that, from the time I'd been little, I'd always tried to keep up with the author. Suspense writing is not unlike the Hansel and Gretel story. One of the versions of that fable is that Hansel dropped smooth stones and Gretel dropped breadcrumbs. The birds ate the breadcrumbs. The mystery/suspense writer is dropping both smooth stones and breadcrumbs. The smooth stones are ambiguous statements, never cheating the reader, but sometimes leading them astray. The breadcrumbs are the real clues to the perpetrator of the crime and the solution of the plot.

I was good at picking up the real clues. I knew why the authors such as the ones I just listed wrote such satisfying mysteries, while other books fell flat at the end. I reasoned that I liked mystery/suspense; I understood it; the first two short stories I sold, "Stowaway" and "Milk Run," were suspense stories. I was going to give the suspense field a try.

"Take a true situation, one that intrigues you, that stays in

your mind, ask yourself two questions, 'Suppose' and 'What if,' and turn them into fiction."

Professor Mowery's advice had never failed me. A sensational murder case in New York had captured everyone's attention. Alice Crimmins, a twenty-six-year-old mother, had been accused of the murder of her two children, a five-year-old boy and a three-year-old girl. She hadn't been accused of criminal neglect, like leaving them unattended and having the house burn down, but of deliberate, coldblooded murder.

It seemed inconceivable to most of us that any woman could do that to her children. And then I thought: Suppose an innocent young mother is convicted of the deliberate murder of her two children; suppose she gets out of prison on a technicality; and then suppose seven years to the day, on her thirty-second birthday, the children of her second marriage disappear?

I liked the premise and decided I'd try to write it. I didn't realize it then, but *Where Are the Children?*, my first bestseller, was in gestation.

My first book, *Aspire to the Heavens*, 1969.

Fourteen

*M*other died on June 3, 1969, four months after *Aspire to the Heavens* was published. Paradoxically, she may have sped her own end by electing to go into a nursing home for a few weeks' rest. After all, she pointed out, she was spending three dollars a month for Medicare and getting nothing out of it. As soon as she began to take it easy, everything in her body slowed up. Her heartbeat became more and more uncertain. I knew it would soon be over when one day, just coming out of sleep, she said drowsily, "Mary, I had the children down to the beach, and Carol wandered off. I couldn't find her. I just don't think I can take care of them anymore." She could no longer take care of others, and she didn't want anyone to have to take care of her.

On June 6, Father Joe Ryan, who had concelebrated her funeral Mass that morning, wrote a note to me. It read, in part:

She was, as I'm sure you realize, one of my favorite people—one of the really beautiful people I've ever known. . . . Someone once said of a friend who had died, "Dying was the first thing he ever did that caused his friends pain." . . . I thought this morning how incongruous it is to be praying for her. If she didn't go straight in, who ever will? It's nice to know that we have an influential friend where it matters most.

P.S. Do you think that the air in heaven is as good as in the Bronx? And if it is, do you think she'll admit it?

Mother had a total of seventeen hundred dollars in insurance from nickel and dime policies she'd paid on for years. They were tied together in an old brown envelope. There was a note to Johnny and me with them. It said, "Don't waste more than a thousand dollars on the funeral. Give one hundred dollars to each of my grandchildren." She didn't realize that she'd already given us all a priceless legacy—her constant devotion and unfailing love.

A month after she died, I wrote in my diary,

And it gets worse. What a year. Tavistock and I on phone a good hour. He said that I'm a historical buff in the space age. My kind of writing was all

wrong for his programs. There was tension be-
tween us.

And on and on and on.

> *I feel degraded, battered, aching, stripped,*
> *robbed, deflated, had. Surely these downward steps*
> *won't continue forever.*

But for the next year it kept getting steadily "worser and worser," as one of the kids used to say. There was no pleasing the guy, or at least *I* couldn't please him. He was still tooting around the country, looking for the right place to settle. Vermont turned out to be full of hippies. Arizona was full of snakes. Wherever he was, he would stop his mobile home at a roadside phone at precisely four o'clock and phone the office.

We all had to be there. Even if you were on a sales call, like Cinderella rushing from the ball at the stroke of midnight, you had to be in place at your desk at precisely 4:00 P.M. each day. And everyone would be in a cold sweat, waiting to see whose head would be on the block that day.

The phone would ring. Laurence, in his capacity as office manager would pick it up. "Hello, G.R." Then he'd call to all of us. "Pick up your phones."

A shout from the other end would send our ear drums vibrating. "IDENTIFY YOURSELVES."

"Hello, Mr. Tavistock. Mary here."

Frank, Don, Barry, Ben . . . etc., etc., etc.

"THE SALES CAMPAIGN IS ALL BITS AND PIECES. IT'S blah, blah, blah . . ." He'd suddenly interrupt his tirade. "HOLD IT A MINUTE."

We waited, knowing the pause meant that he was peeing in the bushes. He had weak kidneys. A moment later we'd hear the sound of the phone being picked up again. "THE SALES CAMPAIGN IS FALLING APART. I DON'T NEED THIS AGGRAVATION. I KEEP THIS BUSI-NESS OPEN FOR YOU KIDS. THAT'S ALL. I KEEP IT OPEN SO THAT YOU'LL HAVE A FINE PLACE TO WORK . . . WAIT A MINUTE."

Back to the bushes.

At the end of the daily castigation, he would sometimes order one or the other of us to pick up the phone in a private office. That person would be his pro-tem new confidante. "I can trust you to know that I'm losing faith in . . ." It was in-evitable that whoever he was losing faith in would soon be ap-plying for unemployment insurance.

The straw that broke the camel's back for all of us was his decision that we would hold one-day meetings in a nearby hotel and tape-record them. Laurence was to express the tape to him overnight, wherever he happened to be. The problem was that if upon listening Tavistock felt that one or the other person was not sufficiently zealous about ideas and plans for the company, that person was on the banana peel express out of there.

We were all off-balance. By then I was forty-one years old,

had worked for Tavistock for five years, and from day to day never knew whether or not I'd be out on my ear with my only skill the rather specialized one of writing his radio programs. I told the others that we were all being intimidated by a guy over a thousand miles away who was making us suspicious of each other every time one of us was told to go into the private room. I said that next time I was ordered to go in there, I wanted everyone else to come in, too. Soon after that, I got my marching orders.

"Mary, go into the private room."

"Certainly, Mr. Tavistock."

I went in, the other five or six of my co-workers at my heels.

"Is the door closed?"

"Yes, it is, Mr. Tavistock."

And it was. The others crowded around me.

"We've got a problem with Laurence," he boomed. "An apple does not look the same from the front as from the back."

I don't know what that statement had to do with Laurence, but it was clear it was his turn in the barrel. At least now Laurence knew what to expect and was able to learn his sins of omission in advance and, to a degree, cover his backside.

I never thought G.R. was stupid. In fact he was a very smart man and very creative. If he hadn't pushed us into out-and-out mutiny, the break might not have come. He sensed something was going wrong in the office and rushed back to New York on the train—he never flew. As he put it, "Jeez, look

what happened to Wiley Post and Amelia Earhart." Pause. "And Will Rogers." But one way or the other, he arrived. Frank and Don and I had had lunch together that day. When we came back to the office, he was sitting at my desk.

I almost fainted, but he smiled benignly. "I admire you, Mary. I admire all of you. You've got spirit. You've got guts. That's what I like. That's what the Gordon R. Tavistock Corporation needs. Now I want you to tell me your problems, and we'll solve them."

I laid out mine: "I've worked for you for five years. I have no sense that I have job security. You've just rearranged the commission basis on the shows I've sold, which means I get a lot less money, and that's after I sold them."

He listened to all of us, nodding solemnly. "We'll have a meeting tomorrow."

The next day he announced the Gordon R. Tavistock plan. He restated that he was only keeping the office open for us kids. He didn't need it. Nothing but aggravation. Now he was going to share the company with us. Starting now, we would go on a point system. As of today, we would get points for shows kept on the air, for expenses kept down, etc. When anyone got x number of points, that person would be entitled to one share of stock in the company.

One share of stock. Nothing was said about the five past years I'd spent there. I did a quick calculation. Based on his timetable, if I was lucky, I'd be eligible for that one share of stock in about a year and a half.

"What do you think, Mary?" he asked.

"I have not words, Mr. Tavistock."

He beamed. "I knew you'd love it."

When I got to the office the next morning, I learned that he'd be in at twelve, and a caterer had been ordered to serve a luncheon to celebrate the new G. R. Tavistock company plan. The caterer arrived, turned my desk into a tabletop, and started putting out the bologna. G.R. made his entrance and heartily greeted all of us.

I handed him my resignation.

"You have another job, Mary?"

"No, but I'm afraid I can't work for you any longer."

At five o'clock he invited me to have a drink. "You're going to open up across the street from me. I know it."

"I don't know what I'm going to do," I replied, which was honest. Frank and Don and I had discussed the possibility of starting out on our own, but nothing definite had been decided.

"If you do, there's room for both of us." The drinks arrived and we clinked glasses. "To a spirit of *cammawaddawy*," he said cordially.

The next morning when I went back to the office to collect my belongings, a burly uniformed guard was sitting at my desk. "The boss says you take nuttin' outta here, lady. Absolutely nuttin'."

In 1975, at my kitchen table, where I wrote *Where Are the Children?* as well as several other of my earliest books.

FIFTEEN

*F*rank and Don and I did start our own company. We called it Aerial Communications. Don didn't stay long, but after a cashless eight months, the company was up and running. Going that long without salary, as well as scraping together five thousand dollars to kick in for start-up costs, had me on the ropes financially. I borrowed on my insurance, hocked my engagement ring and two bracelets Mrs. Clark had left me, and somehow got through it.

Our first office was a one-room sublet on Forty-second Street. We needed a typist, and in response to my phone call to the State Employment Agency, hired a man named Roy on a part-time basis. He was a balding, flabby guy of around forty, with wide, innocent eyes and a baby face. In a hesitant voice, he told me he lived with his mother in the Bronx, did not drink, and could type fast.

The latter was the understatement of the century. He could

practically make the typewriter smoke, and he never seemed to make a mistake. I couldn't understand why he hadn't been snapped up for a typing pool on a full-time basis, because he made it very plain that he wanted to work. I hired him and, lunch bag in hand, he arrived the following morning.

He immediately moved his desk a little to the left so that it was in a direct line with the windowsill. It really didn't matter to me, but I was curious and asked him if there was any particular reason for the move.

His eyes round and guileless, his tone reverential, he said, "Oh, didn't I tell you? The Blessed Mother likes to sit on the windowsill near my desk when I'm working."

Roy lasted with us for about six months, then called in to say he didn't want to work any more and his mother said it was okay to stay home. During those six months, I would steal occasional glances at the window. It was comforting to think that the Mother of God might be blessing our endeavors.

We began to have a healthy lineup of shows and talent. Betsy Palmer, Bess Myerson, Bill Cullen, Arthur Kennedy, Fred Gwynn, Vivian Vance, Lee Merriweather, and Chiquita Banana were among our celebrity hosts. It was a hectic time. Frank and I wore a dozen hats, including writing, selling, producing, and distributing the various series. But as the budget got healthier, we were able to take on additional help.

Those years between 1971 and 1973 were probably among the busiest of my life. David graduated from St. Joe's in '72 and

began his freshman year at Dartmouth College. Now I had one child in law school, two in college, and two in Immaculate Heart Academy. I was starting to make fairly good money, but there never seemed to be enough to cover all the bills.

I was writing a radio show for the actress Peggy Cass at that time and was astonished to learn that she was a sophomore at the Lincoln Center campus of Fordham University. Like me, she hadn't gone to college after high school and wanted to make up for it now.

I decided that if Peggy could be working toward a degree, I could too. She was a busy actress, appearing both in movies and on stage, but she was able to manage it. Carol was seventeen. Patty was fifteen. I could certainly plan to stay in New York for classes after work, and get home late a couple of evenings a week. Broke as I was, I phoned Fordham and got the necessary applications. I think it was the hottest evening in summer 1974 when I took the bus from the office to Lincoln Center to register. There were long lines to sign up for classes, and it was ten o'clock before I finally got my student I.D. photo. My head was slightly tilted to the side and, to put it charitably, I looked dazed, confused, and bewildered. When Johnny saw it, he burst out laughing, and using a voice thick with an Irish brogue said, "I go to church regular, I never so much as drop a dish, and I'd never have a man in my room, ma'am." He was right. From looking at that photo, I could have been typecast as the greenhorn maid in the Broadway hit play *Life with Father.*

The kids got their jollies by buying me bobby socks and warning that if I didn't keep up my marks, they'd rescind my driving privileges.

Johnny's wife, Connie, was very ill with cancer, and she died shortly after I started classes at Fordham. They'd been married less than five years. On the ninth anniversary of Warren's death, I was sitting at Johnny's side in the funeral home. That night in my diary I wrote:

> *I sat there wondering how it had happened to us—I widowed and John widowed. Why so much grief and pain?*

A month later, I received a phone call from a hospital. A voice that barely spoke English said, "Mrs. Clark, I'm sorry to tell you that your brother's dead." John had fallen down the slippery marble steps of his apartment building. He broke his hip but otherwise seemed to be fine; the hospital hadn't picked up the fact that he was bleeding internally. He had just turned forty-three.

Because his death was unexpected, his body was sent to Jacoby Hospital for an autopsy. A driver from the funeral home, Paul Becker's funeral home, of course, drove me there to identify the body. Jacoby had been built on the fields where the three of us used to go sleigh riding. As Johnny's body was wheeled in on a gurney, in my memory I could see Joe setting the pace on his sled. Again I could hear Johnny's voice: *"Isn't this fun, Mare?"*

Little brother, little brother, little brother. The reproach of Margaret and Mary when their brother Lazarus died echoed through me: "Lord, if you had been here my brother would not have died." Mother and Daddy and Joseph and John, I thought. Where does it end? I am the only one left, the last witness to Tenbroeck Avenue.

We got back in the car, and the driver put on a turn signal. "No, please go this way," I directed. We drove up Tenbroeck Avenue and I had him stop for a few moments in front of our house.

Sunday night is my delight . . .

Hahaha . . . I made my Popsicle last . . .

"If you're going sleigh riding, be sure to keep the top button of your coat closed, and watch out for Johnny."

"Be home before dark."

I told the driver, "We can start now."

"This house special to you, or do you know the people who live there?" he asked.

"I knew the people who lived there, and yes, the house *is* special."

The novel I was working on was my hope for deliverance. Every morning I'd go down to the kitchen, pick up the typewriter from the floor in the corner, and set it on the table. Then for a few moments, I'd glory in the feel of the growing pile of pages. I was convinced it was a pretty good story. Finally, after many months, with quiet exultation I wrote "THE END." It was finished.

There was a poem written by a fifteenth-century monk that I keep a copy of on the wall of my Cape Cod house. It expressed my emotion on completion of the novel, and goes something like this: "The book is finished . . . let the writer rejoice. . . . God be praised . . . the book is finished. Instead of a pen, let the writer be given a fat goose. . . ."

I started to retype the manuscript to get a clean copy, but in the process realized I was a long way from the fat goose. The novel needed a ton of work. It was another full year before I wrote in my diary,

I have finished the book and it is good.

I was so sure that I had a saleable manuscript that I vividly remember what I was wearing when I dropped a copy of *Die a Little Death* on Pat Myrer's desk in early September 1973. The title had been inspired by a journal I had read that had been written by a mistress of Louis XIV. When her baby died before it was a year old, she poignantly expressed her grief with these words, "And I with my baby died a little death."

I thought the title was appropriate, since in my manuscript the main character, Nancy, has forced herself to bury in her subconscious the events that preceded the loss of her first two children. If she is to save her new family, however, she must recall those events immediately.

On pins and needles, I kept waiting to hear Pat's verdict. Weeks passed and still no reaction. Finally I got up the courage to phone her. "Did you get a chance to read the man-

uscript?" I asked, fearing what she'd say. She told me she had sent it to the publishing house then known as Harper and Row.

I was stunned. I had fully expected her to tear it apart with suggestions on how to revise it. Pat had been a senior editor with a major publisher before she became an agent, and she often had me rewrite a story before she felt it was ready for submission.

"Then you don't think it needs work?" I asked.

"Absolutely not. It's fine the way it is."

"Then it's going to sell," I told her.

"You can't be sure about that."

"Yes, I can. If you put your imprimatur on it, it's going to sell."

Harper and Row returned it without comment. Delacorte turned it down on the basis that a story of children in jeopardy might upset their women readers.

Here we go again, I thought. Memories of those years of rejection slips for my short stories came flooding back. But then on April 4, 1974, I got an excited call from Pat—Simon and Schuster wanted to buy the novel and had offered three thousand dollars for it.

In my journal I wrote,

At last the dawn breaks through. **Die a Little Death** *sold to Simon and Schuster. I write and do not yet believe. All the trying, the rewriting . . .*

*the feeling of hopelessness. . . . Dear God, the book
has been sold!*

The kids and I called our friends. We had a party going in fifteen minutes. I knew that three thousand dollars wasn't going to make any significant difference in our stretched-thin finances, but that wasn't important. The book had sold.

Then, on July 18, I received another call from Pat. The paperback rights to my novel had been sold to Dell for one hundred thousand dollars. In the journal I wrote,

*Somebody thought enough of my book to pay one
hundred thousand dollars for it. The news came
just after Warrie, Carol, and I had talked about
how broke we are.*

That night we all celebrated at one of our favorite restaurants. Dave was doing a summer term at Dartmouth. Carol called him with the news, and he called back a few minutes later. In honor of the occasion, he had ordered a keg of beer for his fraternity.

That one hundred thousand was split with the hardcover publisher, and, of course, my agent got her commission. But it meant a net to me of forty-five thousand dollars, to be paid over three years, and that extra income took the worst of the choke collar off.

I had compiled a list of all the things I wanted to do in this lifetime and never had a chance to do. Finishing my college

degree topped the list, and now I was doing that. I also wanted to learn how to ski and that winter started to do it, with Joan La Motte Nye, who had lived down the block from me on Tenbroeck Avenue. We'd gone to the Villa together, and for those four years in school, had always tried to sit next to each other in assemblies. We had a running game of trying to make the other laugh at solemn occasions. We still make each other laugh.

That next year after Johnny's death, it was a big help that Joan and I went skiing a number of weekends. We decided that, one way or another, we always seemed to be in uniform together. This time the uniforms were our ski paraphernalia—shopping separately, we'd bought very similar oufits. But this time, instead of oxfords, we had ski boots.

We went to Stowe in Vermont and Hunter Mountain in New York and to smaller slopes in New Jersey. At first I started on the bunny hill, which is the worst possible thing to do. You have three-year-olds cutting in front of you, and if they don't do you in, other beginners will attempt to break your neck by wobbling into you from behind.

One day after a frustrating afternoon on the slopes, we got to the aprés-ski at the lodge, and I told Joan that I felt like an old dog trying to learn new tricks, that I was a hopeless case. She'd been skiing for a couple of years and had made a lot of progress, but it was too late for me.

A good Samaritan at the next table overheard me. "I've been watching you, and you can do it," he said, "but not on the

bunny slope. Tomorrow you've got to go to the top of the middle slope with me." I forget his name. I never saw him after that first morning of going up in the lift and following him down the ski slope, but I bless his memory. He was right; it made all the difference. For the next fifteen years I had a marvelous time skiing—until eventually I smashed my shoulder after, like an idiot, trying my inadequate skill on the expert slope at Sun Valley.

My skiing adventures included going with Joan and Richard to Adelboden in Switzerland. There a horse and carriage picked us up at our gingerbread cottage and brought us to the slopes—another glorious adventure that made me feel a long way from the Bronx.

Another serious item on my list of things to accomplish was to learn how to play the piano. My long-ago stab at it with Miss Mills of our "kitchen privileges" days hadn't stuck. I decided to try it again, but not until after I had gotten my degree from Fordham.

A future item on my list was to have a pied à terre someday in Manhattan. Carol would be leaving for Mount Holyoke College in the fall; Patty would also be in college in two years. Looking ahead, I realized that before too long, I would be facing an empty nest. Rather than having to go home to a lonely house, I thought it would be great to be able to stay in Manhattan a couple of nights a week.

My book was scheduled to come out in August 1975. My first editor at Simon and Schuster felt that *Die a Little*

Death was the wrong title, that it made it sound like a hard-boiled mystery. S&S wanted to position the book as a novel of suspense and suggested I call it *Where Are the Children?* After the title disaster of *Aspire to the Heavens,* I was happy to agree.

Pat Myrer cautioned me to get started on a new book. If this one worked, Simon and Schuster would want another very soon.

Where Are the Children? didn't make the hardcover best-seller list, but it did sell very well and was favorably reviewed. It was optioned by legendary producer Ray Stark for development as a film for Columbia Pictures. I envisioned the premiere in Hollywood, complete with red carpet, flashbulbs, my gracious acceptance of the praise for the fabulous story I had created.

When I got the phone call about the movie option, Warrie and Dave had summer jobs with the Bergen County Mosquito Control Commission and had just come home from a long, hot day killing mosquitos. Hearing my news, they told me they were immediately quitting the jobs and forming an ad hoc committee to save the mosquitos.

But Ray Stark never made the picture. Ten years later, it did at least reach the screen, courtesy of producer Zev Braun. When they were ready to begin shooting on Cape Cod, he asked me to do a cameo in it.

Come! Let us dance to the music of this happy day. As a young girl, I once had won a drama medal at the Villa, and now as a bona fide thespian, I would at last have my day in the sun. I

was cast as a reporter. When the main character, Nancy, is led out of the courthouse after being convicted of murder, I was to lead the pack of baying media types, demanding to know if she'd admit she'd killed her children.

Jill Clayburgh was starring in the film.

"Ready everyone," the director called, then looked at me nervously. "Ready, Mrs. Clark?"

I gave him a thumbs up.

"Action," he shouted.

The camera was on Jill Clayburgh, handcuffed, looking dazed and heartsick as she's half-led, half-dragged by two policemen.

I saw the camera shift to me and rushed across the courtyard. A swarm of local residents hired for the day to depict media types thundered behind me. I shouted, "Come on, Jill, admit it! Did you kill your kids?"

"Cut!"

We all stopped. The director looked at me. "Mrs. Clark, the character's name is Nancy."

I knew it was a good idea I'd stuck to writing.

A great deal of the action for my second suspense novel took place in Grand Central Station. When I was growing up, there had been a radio series on the air called *Grand Central Station*. The tease for the program began like this: "Grand Central Station—crossroads of a million private lives." That was why my working title for the book was *Crossroads*. I was

still writing between five and a quarter of seven each morning, seated at the kitchen table. And once again the manuscript was growing.

The paperback of *Where Are the Children?* came out in June 1976. Dave was graduating from Dartmouth, and we were all heading there for the weekend. A few days before we were scheduled to leave, I got together with writer Lisa Kent, a long-time friend. Lisa suggested that we have dinner in a little restaurant near the Fifty-ninth Street bridge. "They have someone there who reads palms," Lisa said. "I hear she's fabulous."

I put about as much faith in palmists as I do in reading the astrology column in the newspaper, but I went along with the idea. And, truth be told, I had received one startlingly accurate reading during my Pan Am days. In that instance I'd been walking with some of the crew in New Delhi when a Sikh approached me and asked to tell my fortune.

What he predicted became a family joke: "You are going to marry a baldheaded man at Christmastime."

Warren certainly wasn't bald, but he did have a high forehead. I couldn't wait to tell him about the prediction when I got home.

But then the Sikh had added, "You were seeing a man with a mustache. He is very sad that you are betrothed."

I had just received a letter from Jack Kean—"a man with a mustache"—saying he would like to get together, and he urged me to dispense with my engagement. Apparently he and girlfriend number one were kaput—again.

I had told Warren about the letter, and he'd said, "Call this joker up and tell him to get lost." Instead, by my silence, I chose to establish myself firmly as the one who laughs last.

But no question, the Sikh had been on target. I wondered if this new palm reader would come up with anything that even resembled a reasonable prediction.

She read Lisa's palm first. When Lisa came back to the table she seemed impressed. "She's pretty good, Mary."

I went over to her corner. She examined my palms and shook her head. "I don't believe what I am seeing," she told me. "You are going to be world-famous. You are going to make a great deal of money. You will live to be very old, and you will die abroad."

What is this poor soul smoking? I wondered.

The next week, we were up at Dartmouth and wandered into town. The main street there is practically part of the campus, and on it is the Dartmouth Book Store, the oldest bookstore in the country continuously run by the same family. We were browsing through the aisles when Carol grabbed my arm. "Mom, look!"

An enlargement of the advance *New York Times* paperback bestseller list was tacked to the wall. On it was *Where Are the Children?* in the number ten spot.

We floated down the block to the Hanover Inn and ordered champagne.

Maybe that palm reader did know her business.

EPILOGUE

*T*he really big break came a year later. I had turned in the manuscript I called *Crossroads,* which was published under the title *A Stranger Is Watching.*

Along the way I had been giving chapters to Pat Myrer, and under her guidance, the story was as good as I could make it. Simon and Schuster had an option on it, and I was keeping my fingers crossed that the editors would be happy with what I had done and would want to buy it. It seemed to me that I kept reading about people whose first book had done well but whose second had been a dismal flop.

Then, too, there was the old adage that everybody has one story in her or him. Maybe I'd shot my bolt. These were the thoughts that kept running through my mind as I sat at my desk in the Aerial office and wrote scripts for one of our new series.

In April 1977, as I was about to leave for class at Fordham, Pat Myrer phoned. "Are you sitting down?" she asked.

"Yes."

"Get a pencil and write down these figures."

I listened in a daze. Simon and Schuster was offering five hundred thousand dollars for the hardcover rights to the new book; Dell was offering one million dollars for the paperback.

"Think it over," Pat said.

"Think it over!" I shrieked. "Call back and say yes before they change their minds!"

I had three classes at Fordham that evening. I didn't hear one word they said in any of them. I kept writing "one million dollars, one million dollars," over and over again. Then I wrote it again in roman numerals, over and over. I wrote it up and down the page, across the page.

Between classes I called the kids. "Let's plan a trip to Europe," I told them.

My car had one hundred and forty-six thousand miles on it. For weeks I'd been nursing it along, my fingers crossed that it wouldn't break down. With all the tuition payments, there was no way I could think about replacing it.

Floating on air, I left Fordham that glorious evening and got into the car. As I drove onto the Henry Hudson Parkway, the tailpipe and muffler came loose and began dragging on the ground. For the next twenty-one miles, I kur-plunk, kur-plunked, all the way home. People in other cars kept honking

and beeping, obviously sure that I was either too stupid or too deaf to hear the racket.

The next day I bought a Cadillac!

The years since then are many, although they seem few. Financially independent, all of the children out of the house, I remarried in 1978. It was a mistake and lasted just a few years.

The night I received my degree from Fordham, I threw myself a prom. The invitation read: "After lo these many years, Mary Higgins Clark is about to graduate from college. This invitation is twenty-five years overdue. Help prove it's not too late by coming to the prom." The guests were urged to dress as they had dressed for their high school proms. Suggestions: spaghetti straps; a tulle dress; long white gloves; bright red lipstick; feather cuts; borrow the keys to Dad's car.

One of our friends in town had always regretted that he had not driven to his prom in the car he coveted as a kid. In the spirit of my prom, he managed to find that same car and bought it, a 1949 DeSoto. Another friend, mystery writer Ed Hoch, had the evening already committed. He wrote: "Dear Mary, I'm sorry I can't be with you, but in honor of the occasion, at ten o'clock, Pat and I will get in the backseat of the car and neck."

The younger generation raided the attics to find vintage clothing.

There were weddings and grandchildren. Elizabeth was the first grandchild. At the hospital, a nurse told us she was

the baby next to the door of the nursery. In awe, we stood at the window and gushed and cried and pointed out how much she resembled this one and that one in the family. The same nurse came over to us. "Your baby is on the *other* side of the door." We looked, and there she was. If they'd asked me to pick her out among all the babies in the nursery, I could have done it. She was the image of the five babies I had birthed.

After Elizabeth, along came Andrew, and Courtney, and David, and Justin, and Jerry.

When I had five children, a husband, and mother under the same roof, I didn't know I had a small house. When I was living alone, I decided I needed more room. The move to Saddle River, another town in New Jersey, was a happy one. It's a great gathering spot for all of us. The grandchildren can have pool and tennis parties with their friends. I love to look out the window from my study and see them having fun there.

I have my pied-à-terre in Manhattan, overlooking Central Park. On a winter night, I stand on the terrace and imagine so many years ago, my mother, age nineteen, dancing barefoot in the snow.

I had decided that it wasn't for me in this lifetime to ever again experience the wonderful relationship that I knew could exist between a man and a woman. Then in early March 1996,

Epilogue

Patty called me from the Mercantile Exchange where she works. "Have I got a hunk for you," she exclaimed. "His name is John Conheeney. He's been a widower for two years. He lives in Ridgewood." Ridgewood is one of the towns that border Saddle River.

"He was chairman and CEO of Merrill Lynch Futures. He retired two years ago. He's handsome. Everybody thinks the world of him. He's not going around with anybody—I checked. He's told me he's read some of your books. Invite him to the party. I think he'd come."

She was referring to a party I was having on St. Patrick's Day, to celebrate the publication of my then latest novel, *Moonlight Becomes You.*

I invited John Conheeney. He came. He was everything Patty had promised, and more. Eight months later, we were married at my parish church, St. Gabriel's. My five children and six grandchildren and his four children and seven grandchildren filled the front pews. Now, between us, we have sixteen grandchildren. Happily, they all live near us.

There's a wonderful old saying, "If you want to be happy for a year, win the lottery. If you want to be happy for life, love what you do."

I love being a storyteller.

Another definition of happiness is "Something to have, someone to love, and something to hope for."

All my life, these essentials of happiness have been granted to me in abundance, and for that I am deeply grateful.

With John on our
wedding day—
November 30, 1996.
(CHRISTOPHER LITTLE/
CORBIS OUTLINE)

With my wonderful children
Warren, Marilyn, Patty, Care
and David (CHRISTOPHER
LITTLE/CORBIS OUTLINE)